CHRIST UNFURLED

CHRIST UNFURLED

The First 500 Years of Jesus's Life

FR. DAVID VINCENT MECONI, SJ

TAN Books
Gastonia, North Carolina

Cover design by Caroline Green

Cover image: St. Augustine and St. John the Evangelist, 1320-1325, by unknown artist, fresco, Chapel of St Nicholas, Basilica of Saint Nicolas of Tolentino, Tolentino. Italy, 14th century. Bridgeman Images.

Library of Congress Control Number: 2020950368

ISBN: 978-1-5051-1032-6
Kindle ISBN: 978-1-5051-1034-0
ePUB ISBN: 978-1-5051-1033-3

Published in the United States by
TAN Books
PO Box 269
Gastonia, NC 28053
www.TANBooks.com

Printed in the United States of America

To
Fr. Donald J. Keefe, SJ (d. 2018), who
taught me to love the Church,
and
Fr. Leo Sweeney, SJ (d. 2001), who taught
me Christ and the Church are One

"Modern Catholicism is nothing else but simply the legitimate growth and complement, that is, the natural and necessary development, of the doctrine of the early Church."

—St. John Henry Newman, *An Essay on the Development of Christian Doctrine*

CONTENTS

Greater Ones Than These

CHURCH HISTORY AND CHRISTIAN SPIRITUALITY

"Have I been with you so long, and yet you do not know me, Philip? He who has seen me has seen the Father; how can you say, 'Show us the Father'? Do you not believe that I am in the Father and the Father in me? The words that I say to you I do not speak on my own authority; but the Father who dwells in me does his works. Believe me that I am in the Father and the Father in me; or else believe me for the sake of the works themselves. Truly, truly, I say to you, he who believes in me will also do the works that I do; and greater works than these will he do, because I go to the Father" (Jn 14:9–12).

PHILIP CAPTURED THE human heart when he cried out his desire to see and to know God. From the depths of his being, he wanted to behold the fullness of all that is. He instinctually knew that if he could have that, there would really be nothing lacking in his life, and so he begs Jesus: "Lord, show us the Father, and we shall be satisfied" (Jn 14:8). In his response, Jesus assures his followers that faith in him will not only lead to eternal life but will result in even greater works than they see him doing.

How can we do greater things than Jesus? What could Jesus mean here, promising that whoever believes in him will perform greater works than the ones he does? How can Jesus's followers do greater things than the Lord himself?

To ask this question is to open the door to Christ's unfurling himself *into* and *as* his Church. It is to enter into the history of the Church not as a building or even a religion but as an extension of Jesus Christ himself. To pick up a book of Church history, then, is to trace the stories of Christ's disciples as they travel and evangelize, as they gather in worship, and as they set out to defend and clarify the life-giving message Jesus imparted while he walked among them. The first followers of Jesus understood the Church not as an edifice, or as some set of instructions, or even some ceremony, however pious, but as the unfolding of Christ into the lives and lands of those who lived outside first-century Jerusalem. To flip rightly through the pages of the first five hundred years of the Church, then, is to assume a posture of faith that the Church and Christ really are one. In fact, this is precisely how most of the people who feature in the pages to follow understood the body to which they freely belonged. Today, the *Catechism of the Catholic Church* captures such a theology beautifully, officially teaching:

> Christ and his Church thus together make up the "whole Christ" (*Christus totus*). The Church is one with Christ. The saints are acutely aware of this unity: "Let us rejoice then and give thanks that we have become not only Christians, but Christ himself. Do you understand and grasp, brethren, God's grace

toward us? Marvel and rejoice: we have become Christ. For if he is the head, we are the members; he and we together are the whole man. . . . The fullness of Christ then is the head and the members. But what does 'head and members' mean? Christ and the Church" (St. Augustine, *Homilies on the Gospel of John* 21.8). "Our redeemer has shown himself to be one person with the holy Church whom he has taken to himself" (St. Gregory the Great, *Moralia on Job, Preface* §14). "Head and members form as it were one and the same mystical person" (St. Thomas Aquinas, *Summa Theologiae* III.48.2). A reply of St. Joan of Arc to her judges sums up the faith of the holy doctors and the good sense of the believer: "About Jesus Christ and the Church, I simply know they're just one thing, and we shouldn't complicate the matter" (From the *Acts of the Trial of Joan of Arc*).[1]

As such, the Church teaches us today that "the good sense of the believer" never separates Christ from his Church, the Head from his Body. This reality then helps us better understand that the apostles and their immediate successors had no greater access to our Lord than we do today. To the truly Christian mind, every baptism is an unfolding of Bethlehem, every sacrifice is the Passion continued, each consecrated "yes" continues Mary's "let it be done to me according to your word," every feeding of the hungry is to minister to Christ, every pope is an echo of Peter's confession, every woman whose dignity is restored in Christ is

---

[1] *Catechism of the Catholic Church* [hereafter CCC] §795.

another Mary Magdalen, every chalice really is the Holy
Grail.

Whereas Christ could meet a few hundred people at
any one gathering, his Church today gathers billions and
continues to grow. Whereas Christ preached in his native
tongue, his Gospel is today proclaimed in thousands of
languages. Whereas our divine Healer cured the ill and
comforted the mourning throughout only a tiny part of
the Middle East, how many are today healed in his hospitals and nourished in his shelters around the entire world?
Since Truth can never err, perhaps this is how Jesus meant
that we would do "greater things" than if he had remained
on this earth's surface. Whereas Christ founded his Church
on the primacy of Peter (Mt 16:18), the Pentecostal out-
pouring vivified that Church and equipped her with the
languages and growing cultural awareness (Acts 2) of how
to succeed in bringing the Gospel into every land of this
world. So perhaps this is how we are to understand that
bittersweet moment of Christ's revealing his ascension as
being "better" for those he seemingly leaves behind: "Nevertheless I tell you the truth: it is to your advantage that I go
away, for if I do not go away, the Counselor will not come to
you" (Jn 16:7). In ascending, the Son raises all of humanity
into heavenly glory by sending the Holy Spirit, who in turn
makes all his disciples sons and daughters of the same heavenly Father. Christ's departure from us may be mysterious,
it may be confusing, but the virtue of hope knows that in
the end it is better, infinitely better.

In the book of Acts, St. Luke starts a custom of writing down the story of how God's new presence in Christ

changed lives forever. The book of Acts is thus the first narration of the Church's history but was never intended to be a mere history. It is also a theology, a story based in faith that the movement of the first disciples in and out of Jerusalem was something divinely inspired and sustained. This was no mere human endeavor: this was the power of God sweeping through souls and uniting the entire world around the New Adam who has opened the gates of heaven for all. Church history is thus an echo of what Christ began and what Luke and the other apostles continued and extends to the present life of the Church today. Accordingly, these pages approach the genesis and the growth of the Church as the personal entry of the Son of God into the human condition, and then his extending his divine presence throughout the world as his Church. As such, my approach to the first five hundred years of Church history is ultimately the story of Jesus Christ alive and active in his faithful throughout the globe and across the centuries. While some see the history of the Church as the simple chronicling of events or the reporting of dates and deeds, this book understands Church history as the story of how Christ brings cultures and civilizations to a fuller understanding of the Truth that alone sets us free. The Church is neither a building nor a book, but she is instead Jesus Christ's dwelling in and deifying the human soul.

In the following chapters, the Church Fathers will be allowed to speak for themselves on this identity between Christ and Christian. This is a work of both Church history and Catholic ecclesiology, as my overall thesis and consequent methodology maintain that the two cannot be separated. Anything else is just sociology, superficially accurate, perhaps, but nowhere near approaching the depths of Christ at work. This type of study is hence a discipline which demands both an historical awareness of various cultures and significant events—that is the historical—but it is also a species of sacred doctrine which approaches the Church as a body of believers founded and sustained by God himself—that is the ecclesial. Such an approach is, therefore, committed to the view that the Church is a replication of the incarnate God's own human and divine life: heavenly in its essence and organization but all too human in the ones who run and represent the Church's day to day affairs. Accordingly, the first Christian thinkers' words will be reproduced chronologically as we trace the first centuries of Christ and his people.

It was the Lord himself who taught us to see all of history this way. For on the way to Emmaus, the Lord explains to his faithful that to attribute goodness to anyone other than himself would be absurd: "'O foolish men, and slow of heart to believe all that the prophets have spoken! Was it not necessary that the Christ should suffer these things and enter into his glory?' And beginning with Moses and all the prophets, he interpreted to them in all the scriptures the things concerning himself" (Lk 24:25–27). "Beginning with Moses," we learn. Jesus is not present only in the New Testament. All the great stories of liberation and love are ultimately about Jesus Christ, the Messiah who came gently to earth, took on our humanity, and vanquished all that kills and makes life cheap. He came to earth not to live but to die, and in so doing, he defeated death not through power in himself but through obedience to his Father, not through strength but through surrender.

An ancient bishop from modern-day Turkey, Melito of Sardis (d. c. 190) led his people through much of the middle of the second century, dying around AD 180, and helped the Church formulate both a theology of Easter as well as the dating of this movable feast. Through Melito and faithful shepherds like him, the Church continued Christ's hope that in his death and resurrection, we too would see our own humanity hallowed and our own crucifixions consecrated:

> This the one who comes from heaven onto the earth by means of the suffering one, and wraps himself in the suffering one by means of a virgin womb, and comes forth a human being. He accepted the suffering of the suffering one through suffering in a body which could suffer, and set free the flesh from suffering. Through the Spirit which cannot die he slew the manslayer death. He is the one led like a lamb and slaughtered like a sheep; he ransomed us from the worship of the world as from the land of Egypt, and he set us free from the slavery to the devil as from the hand of Pharaoh, and sealed our souls with his own Spirit, and the members of our body with his blood.
>
> This is the one who clad death in shame and, as Moses did to Pharaoh, made the devil grieve. This is the one who struck down lawlessness and made injustice childless, as Moses did to Egypt. This is the one who delivered us from slavery to freedom, from darkness into light, from death into life, from tyranny into

an eternal Kingdom, and made us a new priesthood, and a people everlasting for himself. This is the Pascha of our salvation: this is the one who in many people endured many things. This is the one who was murdered in Abel, tied up in Isaac, exiled in Jacob, sold in Joseph, exposed in Moses, slaughtered in the lamb, hunted down in David, dishonored in the prophets. This is the one who made flesh in a virgin, who was hanged on a tree, who was buried in the earth, who was raised from the dead, who was exalted to the heights of heaven.[2]

From the ancient figures of God's chosen people to the followers of Jesus today, all human encounters with truth and beauty, the legends which recall exploits that free the captive and liberate those bound by sin and scandal, all victories over death tell us ultimately of Christ at work.

It is significant that the earliest known piece of anti-Christian graffiti caricatures a simpleton named Alexamenos worshipping a crucified donkey. It was unearthed in a house which once belonged to the Emperor Caligula (AD 12–41) on the Palatine Hill in Rome, but etched into plaster much later, probably around the year AD 200. The language of ancient Rome's learned class was Greek, and one can imagine the Hellenic haughtiness with which the inscription was written under this pitiful scene: "Alexamenos worships his god." Here hangs an ass on a cross, the perennial

---

[2] From an Easter homily by Melito of Sardis, as in *On Pascha* §66-70, trans. Alistair Stewart (Yonkers, NY: St. Vladimir's Press, 2016), pp. 69–71. This is a most excellent series of English translations of major, mostly Greek, patristic works.

symbol for stupidity and foolishness; this is Rome's way of publicizing the supposed folly of this new band of believers. If this piece of public mockery is any indication, the Romans misunderstood the Christians at first not for being too strong but woefully too weak. The vulnerability of God was something that the pre-Christian world just could not fathom. How could a God deign to rely on a woman for his existence in this world, how could the Almighty dwell within a womb and, above all, how could God die such a disgraceful death before such a peasant crowd? St. Paul was, of course, right: the cross will always be a scandal and a folly to unbelievers (1 Cor 1:23).

The ancient Roman Empire teemed with gods and goddesses. The heavens were packed with powers, while the earth offered myriad cults and creeds seeking to ensure the bounty of harvests and the spoils of war. If a divinity could deliver security and success, the Romans scurried to incorporate such a power into their panoply of supreme beings. In fact, the Romans were particularly adroit at appropriating the numinous lords of the lands they had just conquered: making the ancient pantheon of Athens their own, assimilating the Druids of Britannia, the primal divinities of Egypt, and even securing the many idols of Mesopotamia. Rome welcomed such diversity because this empire alone was secure enough in their own traditions to borrow what they found useful, and strong enough to utterly crush what they found ineffective. They were a practical people, and whatever worked well was most likely assimilated into their way of life. When it came to religion, therefore, the Romans did not care so much about the identity of those being worshipped, as long as each worshipper kept the prosperity of the empire and the well-being of the emperor first in their prayers and sacrifices. As such, interaction with the divine was less about proper doctrine than it was about efficient results.

The Latin phrases *do ut des* (I give to you, so you give to me) and *quid pro quo* (this for that) signify the contractual nature of a religion which was both truly utilitarian and civic in nature. Ancient Romans were the most practical of people, always having the interests of the empire in mind. While the ancient Greeks may have been philosophizing about the perfect avenue for crossing from point A to point B, the Romans were busy building the roads! Their approach to religion was no different. While the Romans certainly interacted with their gods and goddesses, they in no way approached them for a personal relationship or for their soul's sanctification. That is, the idols of Rome were not the kind of beings with whom intimacy was sought or a personal familiarity was fostered. The Romans prayed to the heavenly powers in order to secure imperial victory and common comforts; they were out to secure a universal cult by expanding the number of gods and goddesses available for worship. This state saw in the emperor, known as the "great bridge builder" between heaven and earth, the *Pontifex Maximus,* the representative of all the numinous deities. The emperor's ultimate task was to assuage the gods and goddesses in such a way that they propelled the Roman people forward—ever glorious in battle, enforcing all civic duties, and securing material prosperity. An emperor's success, and thus legitimacy, would be confirmed by his own apotheosis, the recognition of his becoming one now with the heavenly deities upon his death. As such, the strongest of the Roman emperors ruled not only while on earth but even from the skies. The celestial court only continued to grow.

Along the edges of this vast sovereignty, something quite ordinary and unnoticed by most occurred. It was a simple event in a remote place, but it would soon challenge the clout and the very foundations of this supposedly eternal Roman Empire. It happened in the remote region of Palestine, on the eastern edges of the empire. This was the land of the Israelites, the *Iudaei*, as the Latins knew them, a people Rome tended to leave to themselves. Impressing any good Roman, this Jewish race could appeal to the antiquity of their religion, they paid their taxes, were fairly obedient citizens, and kept to a religion based on heredity and not on proselytizing outsiders. The Jews were not a threat to Rome.

But in the backwater town of Bethlehem not far from the ancient city of Jerusalem (*Aelia Capitolina* as the Latin speakers called it), a child was born who was recognized by some Asian astrologers as the one who would rise as the King of the Jews and be the long-awaited Messiah who would gather the scattered tribes of Judah together, challenging Roman rule and reclaiming Palestine as their geographical patrimony. The birth of this helpless little boy not only ignited the local potentate Herod's paranoia but also stirred the revolution at the bottom of every human heart. During the opening decades of the first century, as this baby matured into a man, tradesman, and teacher, he began to attract attention all throughout Judea. He went

about offering a new interpretation of God's original covenant. Some say he even worked miracles. What is clear is
that he offended the wrong religious leaders, striking a fear
so deep within their souls that they turned to an enemy
in whom they hoped to find an ally, the gentiles of Rome.
As the Jewish hierarchy did not have the power to exe-
cute a traitor (the *ius gladii*, or "law of the sword," a right
which the Romans kept for themselves), they looked to the
imperial armies and political leaders to carry out all capital
punishment. To the Jews, this dissident Messiah challenged
their love of the law and polluted their temple; to Caesar,
he was being declared Rome's rival. Jesus had to be put to
death, and in (what came to be reckoned later) the year 33,
he was condemned to the most ignoble death the Romans
had in their arsenal.

For his followers, the crucifixion of Christ completed
the sacrifices of Israel and inaugurated a new way of knowing and loving God and God's people. The gloom of Good
Friday could be understood only in the light of Easter
Morning's radiance. Easter is to the Christian what liberation from Pharaoh was to the Jewish people: foreshadowed
by the Exodus out of Egypt into the Promised Land, the
Resurrection of Christ is the lens through which the first
Christians understood themselves and their entire history as a people stronger than death. For it is ultimately
the resurrection, not the crucifixion, of Christ that formed
this new group of chosen ones. From an empty tomb, the
disciples of Jesus received their identity, and from here, a
new people began to go out from Jerusalem to baptize all
nations in the name of the Father, Son, and Holy Spirit (Mt

28:19). It would not be long until the Romans realized that what had occurred on that new Sabbath was not over and that the witnesses to this event were commanded not to remain silent and still.

This is what those first followers believed, that the Christ had now entered history. The Messiah had been born, the Son of David and the Son of Man. But exactly who was this Savior, and what would this mean for God to have now become one with all of humanity? These are the questions that the next five centuries of Christian life would seek to answer. How this Jesus of Nazareth could be *both* fully the Son of God, eternally consubstantial with his divine Father, *and* just as equally the Son of Mary, conceived consubstantial with his human Mother, would be the life-giving paradox the early Church had to clarify. Originally known as the *People of the Way* (Acts 9:2), these first followers of Jesus Christ believed that their Master had been raised from the dead and had instituted a Church upon the one who seemed to always emerge as a leader of the Lord's first followers, St. Peter.[3]

After the defection of the betrayer Judas Iscariot, the Holy Spirit inspired Peter to initiate the process by which the original eleven brought Matthias into their ranks (Acts

---

[3]   Except for 1 Cor 3:22 and Gal 2:9, Peter is always listed first in the naming of the apostles; he is the first to confess Christ as the divine Son of God, the Messiah who has come into the world (Mt 16:16, Mk 8:29, Jn 6:69), and he is the one who admits that only Christ can have the words of eternal life and any other walk in life is in vain (Jn 6:68); he alone receives the keys to the Kingdom of Heaven (Mt 16:19), and Peter is the first to speak on behalf of this new Apostolic College after Pentecost (Acts 2:13).

1:15–26). These men went about ordaining more and more priests, baptizing more and more households, and cleverly bringing the universality of the Gospel to fit whatever people they encountered, using pagan culture and literature to make the message of Jesus more comprehensible (e.g., Acts 17). Thus appropriating the best of Graeco-Roman civilization, these Christians were not only spreading throughout the empire but also attracting some of the best philosophers, politicians, and people. In response, local governors and prefects sporadically persecuted the Christians, and by AD 64, Christians had become noteworthy enough that the emperor Nero could exploit their novelty as his scapegoat, using the horrific fire in the summer of 64, which ravaged central Rome, as an occasion to persecute these new imperial upstarts.

Here is where this brief introduction to Christian history begins. Using the first four Church councils as signposts, we will traverse the first five hundred years of the Christian story, the first five hundred years of Jesus's life on earth. It is thus to introduce readers to the beginnings of Christ's Church: the development of Sacred Scripture, the ways in which the first Christians began to worship, the attacks they had to endure, the way they prayed, and guidance on how they came to think about God, humanity, and the world. As St. John Henry Cardinal Newman (d. 1890) gratefully came to realize in the *Apologia pro Vita Sua* (*A Defense of his Life*), "To be deep in history is to cease to be a Protestant."[4] What drove Cardinal Newman was

---

[4]   John Henry Newman, *An Essay on the Development of Christian Doctrine* (New York: Image Books, [1878] 1960), p. 35; §5 of his introduction.

not first and foremost the eternal salvation of his Protestant brethren, although that was always on his mind, but it was more a matter of their identity and integrity as Christians belonging—historically and theologically—to the one true Church of Jesus Christ here and now.

Allowing ourselves to be immersed in history, we begin to understand that Christ founded and sustained a Church which was misunderstood and persecuted by the world for its countercultural teachings. We begin to understand how the Lord himself instituted sacraments as channels of his grace, especially the life-giving Eucharist, and we begin to discover this unbroken trajectory from today's Body of Christ all the way back to the original disciples who were ordained to preach the Good News through the whole world. We cease thinking of the Church as a merely spiritual and other-worldly convocation. We refuse to think that the Christian Church arose just a few centuries ago, or that this Body could ever act independently from her Head. The Church is the extension of Christ's very incarnate self, at once both divine and very human, the visible, tangible manifestation of an otherwise invisible God. This is why love of God and love of neighbor are inseparable for the Christian: in taking all of humanity to himself, the Lord has chosen to reveal his person and his plan of salvation through his own members, his holy Church.

As we studiously step into Church history, I would like to argue that we owe special attention to these first few centuries more than any other historical epoch. Any one of us might find ourselves more fascinated by the great doctors of the Middle Ages, or intrigued by modern trends in contemporary theology, but we study patristic theology with a particular solicitude because, as C. S. Lewis once quipped, we cannot intelligently join a discussion at eleven o'clock that began at eight o'clock![5] The Christian faith is organic and holistic, and so all ongoing theology is inherently dependent upon what went before. The Church grows as a child grows: essentially the same being despite her growth in speech, movement, and self-awareness. As she grows, she is able to understand more and more who she is, defend herself from misunderstandings, and go out to others with greater confidence and charity. History moves swiftly, but the Church is the only reality "that frees a man from the degrading slavery of being a child of his age,"[6] because her teachings are not artificial, and so never adapted to meet political popularities. The truths of Christian doctrine are firm while also being flexible. What they are *not* are merely expedient and therefore possibly erroneous.

In the writings of the Church Fathers (and occasionally of some Mothers), we meet the beginnings of Christ's Church. Patristic (from *pater*, the Latin word for father) theology brings us into the only creed professing that at a particular place and point in time, God himself became human and, in so doing, has transformed the human condition forever. Studying the Fathers of the Church introduces us to the workings of the first global and universal

---

[5]   C. S. Lewis's "Introduction" to St. Athanasius's *On the Incarnation*, ed. by an anonymous Religious of C.S.M.V. (Crestwood, NY: St. Vladimir's Orthodox Seminary, [1944] 1989), p. 4.

[6]   From G. K. Chesterton's 1926 essay "Why I am a Catholic," reprinted in G. K. Chesterton, *Essential Writings*, ed. William Griffin (Maryknoll, NY: Orbis Press, 2003), pp. 124–31; 124.

institution ever; in fact, the word "Catholic" comes from two Greek terms: *kata*, meaning "according to," and *holos*, meaning "the whole." This is why theologians down through the centuries are more indebted to previous generations of orthodox thinkers than any scientist or humanist whose genius can change our normal way of thinking and doing things literally overnight. The Church Fathers were commissioned with a truth not their own; they are the first messengers whom we trust and upon whom we build. Turning to the first few centuries of Christianity, we learn how it is precisely here that the Lord Jesus Christ communicated his revelation to the world for all time.

This is a reminder that we are a Church not constricted to the present only. Our Church is ever ancient, founded by Christ himself, and ever new, met visibly today in over a billion people. The Church is both in culture and above it, freeing us from fads and political expedience—*Stat crux dum volvitur orbis*, as the Carthusian motto puts it ("The cross stands steady while the world is turning"). The Church is thus the unbroken continuation of Christ's own incarnate self, the extension of his divine and human presence on earth: divine in her teachings and ability to transform sinners into saints but all too human in her stumblings and scandals in her obvious need for grace. Christ founded a Church because his infinite wisdom understood well that we are a people in need of visibly tangible channels of his otherwise invisible love. This is why God became human and why he founded a Church: in order that post-Ascension people could see, hear, and still touch the Lord. This is why the Church consecrates water, bread and wine, oil, salt and flame; this is why praying while kneeling should feel different than praying standing in adoration or sitting in contemplation; this is why we proclaim Christ's scriptures and communicate his ways in song and in sermon. The visible matters, the body communicates, God has become flesh.

It is this incarnate God who is the subject of John 14:6: "I am the way, and the truth, and the life; no one comes to the Father, but by me." For the Christian, then, the way and the truth and life (the *via, veritas,* and *vita,* in Latin) is no cold dogma, it is this man Jesus Christ. It is in one's surrender and subsequent union that one is saved. It is not merely believing the right thing or even in simply knowing Jesus is the Christ—even the devil can do that: "What have you to do with us, Jesus of Nazareth? Have you come to destroy us? I know who you are, the Holy One of God" (Mk 1:24). Theologians are, therefore, not simply people who talk about God; they must be people who talk to God in such a way that they spend as much time on their knees deep in prayer as they do actively reading and studying. What makes anyone truly a Christian is entering the Church of God freely and consciously, realizing that life here is pure gift. It is sensing deeply that these sacraments, these teachings, this new way of life is who Christ is and now he is unabashedly mine simply because he loves me.

Because he loves us, we Christians also believe that Christ gave everything the human race needed to learn about eternal salvation to his apostles, to the earliest teaching Church. It has been a common belief (what theologians call a *theologoumenon,* a long-standing but unofficial opinion) that revelation came to an end with the death of the last apostle, John the Beloved, approximately in the year 100. In the New Testament's *Epistle of Jude*, we learn that the apostles understood that everything Christ needed to communicate to his Church for their eternal salvation was delivered once and for all to the apostles, referred to there as Christ's holy ones. The holy ones are the Church, the Mystical Body of Christ, on earth still waging the war against evil, in purgatory awaiting the opening of heaven's door, and in heaven where there is only gratitude and joy. The Church was never understood as a building or a set of beliefs in the early years: she was the Bride of Christ, the Holy Gathering, the place where sinners became saints. St. Augustine calls the Church the indispensable half of how Christ understands his fullest self. Like any great lover, Jesus feels incomplete without his Bride, a Head without a Body. That is why Church history is an essential part of our growth in holiness: to see how we sheep are never without a shepherd, how we belong to this glorious family, and how we have access now within our very souls to the Lord and Lover of all, Jesus Christ.

Patristic theology thus aims to foster a sort of ecclesial devotion. The Church as founded by Jesus Christ is the continuation of his own divinely human, or humanly divine, life. He is the Son of God who took on human flesh and chose to live among us as one of us. If it were not for the Church he so intentionally and desirously started, Christianity would be nothing more than exercise in historical recall. We would be doomed to remember a Jesus who once lived, or maybe we could look forward to a Jesus who will come again. But in and through his Church, the life-giving

Body and Blood of Jesus continue to be with us in the Most Holy Eucharist. The merciful forgiveness of Jesus himself is still available in the sacrament of Reconciliation. The Descent of the Holy Spirit at Pentecost continues in every sacrament of Confirmation, and of course, followers of Jesus continue to enjoy the rebirth he insists upon (see Jn 3:3) in the initiating gift of the sacrament of Baptism. His words continue to be heard and preached upon (as well as studied) in the Holy Scriptures, and his faithful still gather daily in prayer and in song. Jesus has not left this world, but he has continued with us as the Head of the Body, as the Lover comes to his Beloved—in one flesh and one spirit.

This Mystical Body grows, however, in a very special way. It does not grow artificially by grasping for things outside of it in order to make it look more up-to-date and more relevant to an ever-changing world. In the New Testament's *Epistle of Jude*, we learn of this Jude who presents himself as "a slave of Jesus Christ and brother of James" (Jude 1:1). This Jude communicates to his beloved audience that "being very eager to write to you of our common salvation, I found it necessary to write appealing to you to contend for the faith which was once for all delivered to the saints" (Jude 1:3). From this passage and from sacred tradition, Christians have always held that everything we need to possess and to live in Christ forever, "our common salvation," was handed down "once and for all" to those to whom Christ wanted to communicate his teachings. All teaching thereafter—every papal pronouncement, every piece of Church teaching—must be an explication or an unfolding of what we have already received "once for all."

Since the Christian faith is an organic and not an artificial reality, it is something which grows from within, not something that is added to from without. This understanding of what is called the "deposit of faith" was given whole and entire to the apostles by Christ himself; future understandings of those truths will only deepen but never differ from what Christ originally imparted to his apostles. This is why, by the middle of the fifth century, a former French soldier turned Christian theologian and monk, St. Vincent of Lérins (d. c. 445), could use "antiquity" for one of the essential hallmarks of orthodoxy. In his guidebook for detecting true doctrine, Vincent laid out three criteria for judging whether a Christian doctrine or an interpretation of Sacred Scripture was developing authentically or heretically. In the opening of his *Commonitorium* (a title meaning to prompt or instruct the memory), Vincent summed up much patristic theology when he taught:

> In the Catholic Church herself we take the greatest care to hold that which has been believed everywhere, always and by all. That is truly and properly 'Catholic,' as is shown by the very force and meaning of the word, which comprehends everything across the world. We shall hold to this rule if we follow universality, antiquity, and consent. We shall follow *universality* if we acknowledge that one Faith to be true which the whole Church throughout the world confesses; *antiquity* if we never depart from those interpretations which our ancestors and fathers in the Faith proclaimed; *consent*, if in antiquity itself we keep

following the definitions and opinions of all, or certainly nearly all, the bishops and doctors alike.[7]

So, as time passes, we see a general consensus developing within Christ's Church that what his believers must hold true will always be universally accepted, apostolically ancient, and consented to consistently by the People of God. Again, this is why Church history matters; it provides us with a reliable guide into millennia of illuminating Christian doctrine, generations of passionate saints, and an ever-growing awareness of who God is and how he interacts with his beautiful creation.

In the pages to follow, we shall proceed chronologically, moving from the year 100 up to the middle of the fifth century. Chapter 1, "Preludes and Persecutions," takes up the question of why the first followers of Jesus were mercilessly maltreated and brutally tortured. How did they respond and how did these first Christians accordingly organize themselves? What was the "Church," the *ecclesia*, a word meaning "to be called" (*cleo-*) "out" (*ex-*) of the world and into a new way of life? The first generation of theologians we shall examine are known collectively as the Apostolic

---

[7] St. Vincent of Lérins, *Commonitorium* §2.6; trans., C. A. Heurtley, *Nicene and Post-Nicene Fathers*, vol. 11 (Peadbody, MA: Hendrickson Publishers, [1894] 2004), p. 132. While these nineteenth-century translations can be sometimes stilted, the series of patristic texts edited as *Ante-Nicene Fathers* and *Nicene and Post-Nicene Fathers* (in the second edition with Henry Wace), overseen mainly by Philip Schaff, a Swiss-born Protestant Church historian (d. 1893), these reprinted volumes make otherwise relatively obscure texts conveniently handy. The entire series can be found gratis under the "Fathers" tab at www.newadvent.org. We shall quote from this thirty-eight-volume series whenever its English translation would be the most available today.

Fathers. The works considered will range from the writings of St. Clement of Rome (88–99), to the letters of Ignatius of Antioch (martyred around 107), all the way through the *Epistle of Barnabas*, a letter attributed to the apostle but most likely a much later forgery. We learn from these initial Christian texts the ways in which the earliest followers of Jesus organized worship, ordered their days and times of prayer, and grew to understand who they were as a living and certainly expanding community. We also receive good basic doctrine regarding the person of Christ and our new life in him. But this new life resulted in the imitation of their Founder, even unto death, and very early on we are provided with acts of the famous martyrs whom Catholics still recall in the Roman Canon of the Mass.

Chapter 2, "Apology, Acceptance, and the Council of Nicaea," opens in the middle of the second century when martyrdom was still very much a reality. But with the writings of Justin Martyr, a new genre of Christian literature begins, the Apology. Originally, "apology" was a Greek term meaning the use of reason to defend oneself from an unjust criticism.[8] What makes the latter part of the second century so unique is that here we see Christian theologians begin to relate the Greek philosophy of the day (mainly

---

[8] For example, in 399 BC, Socrates delivered his famous *Apology* upon death as he sought to defend himself from the censors of Athens, murderously upset that this great philosopher would challenge the polytheism of his day; in 1864, John Henry Cardinal Newman, after having been received into the Roman Catholic Church, wrote his great *Apologia Pro Vita Sua* to defend himself from the condemnations of those in the Oxford Movement who saw in Newman's love for the ancient Faith an unpatriotic act of rebellion.

Plato's way of seeing the cosmos and the soul) to the Christian Scriptures in order to make the faith more accessible and illuminating to those still unfamiliar with Jesus and his Church. Over time, this writing legitimized the Faith in the eyes of pagan thinkers, and by the early fourth century, the emperor himself puts an end to anti-Christian laws and legalizes the Church, allowing her to worship publicly, own land, and gather openly without fear of retribution.

In fact, that emperor, Constantine, is so concerned about ecclesial unity that he convenes the first ecumenical council in order to formulize basic Church teaching. Chapter 3, therefore, opens with a look at the context in which the Council of Nicaea took place and then moves on to that of Constantinople and the richness of fourth-century theology, highlighting those theologians best known as the Cappadocians. Christianity was a thoroughly Greek enterprise for centuries: The Church prayed and sang in Greek and theologians illuminated the central Christian mysteries not only in the language of Greek but with very Hellenistic concepts. Astutely trained men like Basil of Caesarea (d. 379), his brother Gregory of Nyssa (d. 395), and their cherished friend St. Gregory of Nazianzus (d. 390) were the thinkers of this period and helped develop the Church's teaching on the Trinity, formulating God's very life as one substance in three persons. This would be hammered out and put into a final creedal formula at the First Council of Constantinople in 381, when the Cappadocians helped the whole Church clarify the most proper articulation of the mystery of the Trinity.

By the year 400 the Church in the Latin-speaking West and North Africa had come into her own, producing men like Hilary of Poitiers (d. 368), Bishop Ambrose (d. 397), Jerome (d. 420), and St. Augustine. In Chapter 4, therefore, we shall turn to how these great Fathers of the Church explained the Christian life and what contributions they made to the ongoing treasury of Catholic doctrine. We shall focus our thoughts here around St. Augustine of Hippo (354–430) as it is nearly impossible to overestimate what he gave the Church in terms of example and erudition. Chapter 4 brings us through the Council of Ephesus in 431 and all the beautiful theology that emerged from that fourth ecumenical council. Here the Church declares Mary the Mother of God, and we will see how theologians such as Cyril of Alexandria and Proclus of Constantinople worked hard to secure this title which Christians had been using for quite some time already.

We then travel from Ephesus to the Council of Chalcedon in 451. In Chapter 5, our attention is on Pope Leo (440–61) and his writings on the person of Jesus Christ. Whereas the first two councils, Nicaea and I Constantinople, dealt mainly with the life of the Trinity, Ephesus and Chalcedon turned more intensely to the person of Christ himself and seek to show how he can be both fully God and fully human. These Chalcedonian deliberations helped to clarify not only questions regarding God's nature but also the role of humanity and the glory of what it means to be a creature assumed to or deified by the divine. We, therefore, conclude our brief study by taking up the theology of the Council of Chalcedon and looking at Pope Leo of Rome and how that ancient Apostolic See provided the teaching and unity needed to keep Christ's Body one in mind and heart.

They Will Also Persecute You

PRELUDES AND PERSECUTIONS (100-313)

*"Remember the word that I said to you, 'A ser-
vant is not greater than his master.' If they persecuted me, they will persecute you; if they kept my
word, they will keep yours also" (Jn 15:20).*

JUST AS ROMAN officials and Jewish leaders came to despise
Jesus of Nazareth, they would surely do the same to his followers. He told them in no uncertain terms: if you belong to
me, the world will hate you. This is a hatred brought about
by the identity forged in love between Christ and Christian:
"If the world hates you, know that it has hated me before it
hated you. If you were of the world, the world would love
its own; but because you are not of the world, but I chose
you out of the world, therefore the world hates you" (Jn
15:18–19). This is a sad reality traceable back to Cain and
Abel: the cruel condemn the kind, the guilt of the unrigh-
teous man propels him to destroy the just, the spiritually
malformed destroy the virtuous so as to feel better about
their own self-imposed ugliness, and the fearful malign the
magnanimous so their own pettiness is never confronted.

As the man of Truth, Jesus Christ was an offence against
the Roman Empire, the nation which could allow no other
king than Caesar (Jn 19:15). It was in this violent clash that
Christianity would grow, and it is here we now turn.

When the writing of Sacred Scripture came to a close,
conveniently dated usually around AD 100, the Church
was commissioned with explicating the meaning of everything Christ wanted to communicate to the world. The
canon of Scripture became precisely that, the "measuring
stick" (in Greek, *kanon*) by which the developing Church
would come to measure what she considered true doctrine
and proper worship. Even though this process of adjudicating which books belonged in the biblical canon was
centuries in the making—the final form of the Bible as we
have it today was not decided upon officially until the late
fourth century—the first group of Christian theologians
chronologically after Paul and the Gospel authors became
known collectively as the Apostolic Fathers. These writings
were so revered in the second and third centuries that they
were often considered divinely inspired by some and even
for a time were proclaimed liturgically, erroneously giving
them the same status as biblical writings. But as the Church
developed, these writings were removed from the Mass and
were afforded an important but no longer inspired place in
the formation of Christian theology.

There is no settled list on what exactly constitutes the
writing of an Apostolic Father, but generally these are
documents which appeared anytime between the late first
century up through the middle of the second century and

typically include (but not always limited to) these seven works:

The *Epistles of Clement of Rome* (d. 99)
The *Didache* (late first century)
The seven *Epistles of Ignatius of Antioch* (d. 107)
The *Epistle of Barnabas* (late first and early second century)
The *Epistle* and *Martyrdom of Polycarp* (d. 160)
The *fragments* of Papias of Hierapolis (d. 163)
The Shepherd of Hermas (composed throughout the second and maybe third centuries)

In some ancient collections, the anonymously written second-century *Epistle to Diognetus* and the text of Quadratus of Athens (d. c. 130) are included in this list, but given the clearly apologetic tone of these two writings, we shall include them in the next chapter when we look at more explicit defenses of the Faith.

The writings of the Apostolic Fathers are generally not sophisticated intellectual analyses. Rather, they consist of practical instruction for the conduct, organization, piety, and obedience required of a Christian. As those who had chosen to follow Jesus were realizing that the world's end was not as imminent as some had originally thought, the basic elements of the Christian story were now being clarified as was its organizational life. Hence these writings include Church manuals on how to conduct oneself very practically in prayer and worship, martyrial acts displaying the heroic deeds of those who were being persecuted for living this faith out publicly, and letters from episcopal authorities directing the dating of major feasts and the conduct Christ willed for those who bore his name.

This chapter is accordingly divided into two main sections. In the first section, we shall explore the time around the year 100 in order to see what kinds of writings were being produced, what themes were important to the first generations of Christians, and what they faced as they left Jerusalem and entered the oftentimes hostile world of the Roman Empire. In so doing, we shall learn how the writings of these Apostolic Fathers display our main thesis; namely, that the doctrine of the Mystical Body develops historically as Christians gradually come to understand themselves as the Church, as envoys and extensions of Christ's very presence in the world. While this doctrine will be explicated more fully in the centuries to come, it is a constant and steady seed planted in the Incarnation, rooted in Scripture, and beginning to flower in the writings we shall next explore. The second section of this chapter then takes up the scriptural promise quoted above that those in whom Christ lives will be hated and persecuted in this world. The persecutions of Rome became for the early Church hardly an extinguishing ultimatum but instead proved to be the spark that ignited a fire which could not be contained.

According to the "Father of Church History," Eusebius of Caesarea (c. 260–c. 340), Emperor Diocletian enacted a three-fold line of attack in his effort to eradicate Catholicism from the empire: to bring to rubble all Christian places of worship, to punish Church leaders, and to set in flames the Bible's pages. We learn from Eusebius's *History of the Church* that in the year 303, Diocletian issued an imperial decree and had it published everywhere, "ordering the churches to be razed to the ground and the Scriptures destroyed by fire, and giving notice that those in places of honour would lose their places, and domestic staff, if they continued to profess Christianity, would be deprived of their liberty. Such was the first edict against us. Soon afterwards other decrees arrived in rapid succession, ordering that the presidents (*proedros*) of the churches in every place should all be first committed to prison and then coerced by every possible means into offering sacrifice."[9]

One of the Church's fiercest enemies and a great strategist and urban planner in his own right, Diocletian (244–311) understood that if the Christian faithful were going to flourish, they would need a clear identity of their own leaders, places to gather, and sanctioned pages from which to proclaim and teach a unified message. This great schemer accordingly pressured the visible face of the Church to offer sacrifice to the Roman gods in the hopes that the faithful would see the fickleness and cowardice of their leaders and apostatize as well.

But the opposite seemed to happen. As Tertullian (c. 155–c. 240) knew and so memorably put it, the martyrs' blood had become the seed of the Christians (*semen est sanguis Christianorum*).[10] So, as the Christian body grew, adaptations to circumstances inevitably had to be made. To safeguard Jesus's authentic mission and message, Church

---

9   Eusebius, *The History of the Church*, 8.2; trans. G. A. Williamson (New York: Penguin Classics, [1965] 1989), p. 259.
10   Tertullian, *The Apology* §50.13; *Corpus Christianorum Latinorum* 1.171. This series is used by scholars for the most critical and up to date Latin editions we currently have for the Western Church Fathers.

leaders scurried to put into place three guiding principles first formulated in the Apostolic Fathers: (1) the monoepiscopacy and the proper determinants for apostolic succession; (2) an ongoing "Rule of Faith," an umbrella term which guided how Christians should pray, fast, organize Church structures, conduct themselves in Roman society, and so on; and (3) the canonicity of Scripture—which books belonged in the Bible as divinely inspired and which ones did not? Using these three key principles, the first section of this chapter thus examines how the earliest generations of bishops and theologians understood Church leadership and practice.

Preludes: The Apostolic Fathers

As mentioned, the first ones to face the question of how the Church should faithfully expand are known collectively as the Apostolic Fathers, a seventeenth-century term coined to describe these leaders who lived and wrote immediately after the age of the first apostles. For the most part, these Apostolic Fathers shepherded communities consisting of Jewish converts who sought to bring Middle Eastern Monotheism in line with Greek philosophy so as to make the message of Jesus Christ alive and applicable to a larger world. These Apostolic Fathers emerge from this convergence of cultures as reliable guides who helped navigate the Lord's barque through the bloody storms of persecution, setting a course toward the early Church councils, and finally into the more tranquil harbor of an empire ready to hear the Good News of Christ. They were all Greek speakers; most of them were trained rhetoricians and had proven to be the empire's best students of law and grammar. But these men detected something beautiful, something true in the new way of life exhibited by the Christians around them. They witnessed the lives of other Christians, they studied this new Way, they were convinced and so converted to Christ, they presented themselves for Baptism and the sacraments, and then rose to become the direct successors of the apostles, the first generation of bishops of the post-apostolic Church.

When we examine the writings of these first post-biblical authors, we begin to detect how the union between Christ and Christian, between Christ and Church, appears in these early writings. As a key tenet in the Faith Christ handed on to his Church, this theology of the Mystical Body in every age must necessarily be detected. Yet it is also true that this doctrine will be treated in different authors with varied levels of lucidity and vigor. Robust theology and the elucidation of dogma were not the main concerns of the following authors. The Apostolic Fathers were more concerned with helping Christ organize his Church and order the more pragmatic elements of the liturgical and social lives of his faithful followers. Yet even in these Church manuals and practical exhortations to holiness, we shall come to see how the first ecclesial communities across the Mediterranean stressed, if even faintly, the need for unity between Christ and his Church so as to eschew internal division and succeed in bringing the Gospel out into the rest of the world.

What is at stake in tracing the history of Christ's Church in this manner is to see how his faithful stewards were building up a canon, an officially approved treasure chest, from which they could cite ecclesial practices, saints to emulate, and theological doctrine to trust. The term "canon" originally meant a "measuring stick" ("rule" in Latin), and so began to be used throughout the second century to describe what was acceptable and what was outside the boundaries of right religion. The early Church needed to have an ongoing guide informing her what persons and practices could be trusted. This ongoing appropriation and consistent reliance upon certain figures and ways of worship helped the nascent Body of Christ know how sacraments should be performed, what ascetical practices should be implemented, what feasts should be celebrated and when, what the best methods and postures for prayer might be, and so on.

St. Clement of Rome (d. 99)

Despite some chronological murkiness, there is strong agreement that the first in the list of Apostolic Fathers is St. Clement, the fourth bishop of Rome (after Peter [33–64], Linus [64–76], Anacletus [76–88]), ruling from sometime in 88 until his death on November 23, 99. There are two documents related to Pope Clement: the earlier *Epistle to the Corinthians* is authentic and dates usually to 96, but the so-called *Clements' Second Epistle to the Corinthians* is not an epistle but a homily, nor was it written by Clement but is an act of later forgery.

From his position of early papal authority, Clement began to universalize the earliest doctrines and dating of Christian feasts we still enjoy. As the thesis of our history purports, unity between Christian and Christ and between all Christians is one of the strongest messages of Pope Clement's homily. Schism is an assault against the Body of Christ. In the Christian story, unity and charity are synonymous, and any division—moral, personal, or doctrinal—is to be overcome through the grace of the Holy Spirit. In Clement's writing, the Greek term for "one mindedness," *homonoia*, appears often, stressing how the mind of Christ must become the mind of all Christ's followers.

This is why Jesus teaches each of us to pray "*Our* Father," because none of us do anything apart from the Body of Christ in whom we have been claimed. Pope Clement, therefore, uses his august position as the bishop of Rome to demand that divisions in Corinth cease, "the odious and unholy breach of unity among you, [which] hot-headed and unruly individuals have inflamed to such a pitch that your venerable and illustrious name, so richly deserving of everyone's affection, has been brought into serious disrepute."[11] Charity is the only real virtue that binds individuals together truly and eternally, and Clement insists that all persevere in unity and to let love be the virtue which ties them together: "And over all these put on love, which binds everything together in perfect harmony" (Col 3:14). What is also significant to see here is how early one particular

---

[11] *The First Epistle of Clement to the Corinthians* §1, as in *Early Christian Writings*, trans. Maxwell Staniforth (New York: Penguin Books, 1987), p. 23.

bishop already sees himself as a universal arbiter and peace-maker. Clement's parochial concerns include Corinth because the pope's diocese is not bound by the city walls of Rome.

This exchange between Clement and the Corinthians reflects one of the most foundational struggles the early Church had to clarify and ratify: Who speaks for the community? Who is the official voice among all the disparate opinions and tendencies? Who will determine the major moments and celebrations of a body that should be coordinated not just in the same town or country but in the entire world the Lord has saved? As an institution founded by Christ (Mt 16:18), this nascent Church responded rightly only when Christ's voice could still be discerned clearly and thus obeyed properly. As such, the monoepiscopacy arose, one bishop shepherding one diocese, a major factor ensuring proper growth at the turn of the second century.

This is why the first half of Pope Clement's letter traces how the Lord unifies his people under the humble surrender of one faithful personin each epoch: Abraham, Moses, Lot, Job, and even Rahab. Each of these biblical heroes shines forth as prefigurements of the lowly Lamb Jesus Christ who offered himself to the Father in order to unify all peoples into the heavenly kingdom. This is the sole purpose of his Church: to bring peoples of diverse races and ways of life into an integrated harmony, here on earth initially, but ultimately and most completely in heaven. Clement draws from the image of gluing otherwise disparate pieces together to form something beautiful. That is why he exhorts the Corinthians to "attach" themselves to the holy faithful in the Church: "So let us attach ourselves firmly to men who have received this grace. Let us clothe ourselves in a mutual tolerance of one another's views, cultivating humility and self-restraint, avoiding all gossiping and backbiting, and earning our justification by deeds and not by words."[12] Such charitable deference toward our neighbor is possible only through the grace of Christ who himself gives us the perfect pattern of love.

It is only through incorporation—coming into the *corpus*—into the Body of the Lord that we come to understand the reality of all things. Clement draws an unbroken arc between creation and salvation, teaching that the unity desired in and by Jesus was first hinted at when God brought all humans out of nothing:

> In Christ Jesus, then, let this corporate body of ours be likewise maintained intact, with each of us giving way to his neighbor in proportion to our spiritual gifts. . . . For just consider, my brothers, the original material from which we took our being. What were we, pray, and who were we, at the moment of our first coming into the world? Our Maker and Creator brought us out of darkness into His universe as it were out of a tomb; even before our birth He was ready with His favours for us. To Him we owe everything, and therefore on every count we are under the obligation to return thanks to Him.[13]

---

[12] Ibid., §30; Staniforth, *op.cit.*, p. 35.
[13] Ibid., §38; Staniforth, *op.cit.*, p. 38.

This we learn is the entire plan of God in structuring a people unto his own self, to love and to be loved: "It was in love that all God's chosen saints were made perfect; for without love nothing is pleasing to him. It was in love that the Lord drew us to himself; because of the love he bore us, our Lord Jesus Christ, as the will of God, gave his blood for us—his flesh for our flesh, his life for our lives."[14]

As the decades unfold, this gratitude—*eucharisto* in Greek—will be more and more explicitly linked to the unity of the Eucharist, that primal Christian celebration. God's newly-chosen people literally see and hear and taste their Lord's enfleshment, an incarnation achieved only through the gathering of otherwise disparate materials into a life-giving unity.

The Didache

An important development in this type of formation was the early composing of Church manuals, and a very early and important example is known as the *Teaching*, or the *Didache* in Greek. Anonymous in its authorship and unsure in its dating, this recently discovered document (unearthed extant only in 1873) is now generally agreed to have come from the late first century. The *Didache* is important not only for its antiquity but also because it provides a unique insight into how a very early generation of Christians, probably in modern-day Syria, were being taught to live and to pray.

It instructed the first Christians how to pray and act properly, providing foundational structure for future

---

14   Ibid., §49; Staniforth, *op.cit.*, p. 43.

documents concerning Church order. This is a short document filled with mandates for worship and practice. For example, "Do not keep the same fast days as the hypocrites. Mondays and Thursdays are their days for fasting, so yours should be Wednesdays and Fridays."[15] As is the case with most of these treatises, how to conduct the Eucharist properly was also a central concern, but the *Didache* ventures to provide the earliest rationale regarding the reason the Lord intentionally used bread as the means by which he would consecrate and convey his Body. Again, we see this is a matter of unity, and such communion must be intended by all participants who present themselves to receive the Body of Christ: "As this broken bread, once dispersed over the hills, was brought together and became one loaf, so may thy Church be brought together from the ends of the earth into thy Kingdom. 'Thine is the glory and the power, through Jesus Christ, for ever and ever.' No one is to eat or drink of your Eucharist but those who have been baptized in the Name of the Lord; for the Lord's own saying applies here, 'Give not that which is holy unto dogs.'"[16]

This is the first theology of why the Lord chose explicitly and irrevocably bread and wine at the Last Supper, prepared for centuries by his Jewish ancestors: bread and wine are foods which are brought about through the process of unification. By bringing many grapes into one and many grains into one loaf, the *Didache* argues that this process symbolizes the ecclesial unity meant for all Christians now gathered into one body. We can see how post-biblical

---

[15]   *Didache* §8; Staniforth, *op. cit.*, p. 194.
[16]   Ibid., §9; Staniforth, *op. cit.*, pp. 194–95.

theologians take what they had learned about what Christ did and apply reason and experience to come to a deeper understanding of his person and his actions. Here, for instance, the Lord uses bread and wine for the Eucharistic Liturgy because they are products of individual realities (e.g., grains of wheat and grapes) and in Christ's hands are brought together into a wonderful whole—just as Christians, though many, become one in the Lord's Mystical Body, the Church.

The areas proper to theology and the way to do theology properly were of great concern to the Church's first leaders because they knew they had been commissioned to lead Christ's people into heaven. Note how this beautiful theology of unity assumes ecclesiastical discipline: the Eucharist is the result of the baptized vocation, and only those in proper standing with the Church are able to receive Jesus validly. Whereas later Reformers criticized the Catholic Church for this "closed communion" table, as they called it, we see how this is not a later imposition or some medieval accretion. When Jesus commanded the apostles to "do this in remembrance of me" (Lk 22:19), he did not thereafter provide many specifics. But the apostles and their successors trusted that how the Church would act and pray would ultimately be guided by the Holy Spirit's leading them into more and more truth (Jn 16:13). This beautiful text thus closes with lengthy descriptions on how baptism is to be performed and how the Eucharistic prayers are to be conducted. As such, it stands as the earliest manual of Church practice, laying the foundation for later codes of law and ecclesial constitutions.

Ignatius of Antioch (d. 107)

It is intriguing to learn that those who followed this truth freely were called "Christian" for the first time in Antioch (Acts 11:26), since Antioch is also the place where these men and women were called "Catholic" for the first time:

> Abjure all factions, for they are the beginning of evils. Follow your bishop, every one of you, as obediently as Jesus Christ followed the Father. Obey your clergy too, as you would the Apostles; give your deacons the same reverence that you would to a command from God. Make sure that no step affecting the church is ever taken by anyone without the bishop's sanction. The sole Eucharist you should consider valid is one that is celebrated by the bishop himself, or by some person authorized by him. Where the bishop is to be seen, there let all his people be; just as wherever Christ is present, we have the catholic Church.[17]

This theme of ecclesiastical unity and the Christian people thereby forming the Mystical Body of Christ is central to each of the seven extant letters we have from Bishop Ignatius, as he is being dragged from his see in Antioch to his martyrdom in Rome in 107.

Ignatius of Antioch argued that constitutive of Christian sanctification was "uniting in a common act of submission and acknowledging the authority of your bishop and clergy."[18] Ignatius was a firebrand responsible for shifting

---

[17]   *Letter to the Smyrnaeans* §8; Staniforth, *op. cit.*, p. 103.
[18]   *Letter to the Ephesians* §1; Staniforth, *op. cit.*, p. 61.

the culture from the practices of ancient paganism to the new ways of Christianity, and those in power needed him gone. So around the year 107, the emperor Trajan (98–117) sent ten soldiers, whom Ignatius teasingly referred to as "panthers" who "only grow more insolent the more gratuities they are given,"[19] to bring the great bishop of Antioch to Rome to die in the Flavian Amphitheatre. There was no doubt in Ignatius's mind that his forced journey across Asia would be his last. He therefore reached out to the major Christian dioceses between Syria and Italy, composing letters to the People of God in these places exhorting them to stay close to their bishop. In this way, they might avoid the hubris and arrogance that inevitably comes from theological novelty and pitting one's own self against the community.

Our word for the devil refers to a name Ignatius of Antioch understood all too well, seeing how the term "diabolo" comes from the Greek word for throw, *ball-ein* (from which we obviously get the word "ball," and other great words like sym-bol, hyper-bole, and so on). The Greek prefix to scatter is *dia-* (which we can hear in the terms dia-stolic or dia-spora), and so the word "diabalo" means the one who seeks to foster disunity, to scatter Christ's sheep into a fearful disarray. The antidote against this dispersion for Ignatius was the bishop's divinely-commissioned responsibility of ensuring ecclesial unity and, thus, true worship: "That is why it is proper for your conduct and your practices to correspond closely with the mind of the bishop . . . attuned to

---

[19]   *Letter to the Romans* §5; Staniforth, *op. cit.*, p. 86.

the bishop like the strings of a harp and the result is a hymn of praise to Jesus Christ from minds that are in unison."[20]

Ignatius composed these letters as he was dragged to Rome to die, insistent that as God took on visible earthly unity in Christ, all Christians must also be visibly united in the same body, the Catholic Church. Such unity is nowhere more apparent than in the worship offered around a common altar. For the Apostolic Fathers who choose to write about it, the Eucharist appears in these early years as the ongoing fulfillment of Jesus's promise to be with his people always (Mt 28:20) and never to leave them orphans (Jn 14:18). How is the incarnate Lord still with us on earth? The incarnate God has chosen to dwell in us not merely spiritually, for that is the prerogative of the Holy Spirit. It is utmost fitting, then, that Jesus's life-giving body and blood remain available for those who lived after AD 33, and the great theologians of the Christian tradition—Ignatius of Antioch especially—have always pointed to the Eucharist as the way Christ continues his holy presence among us: "Make certain, therefore, that you all observe one common Eucharist; for there is but one Body of our Lord Jesus Christ, and but one cup of union with his Blood, and one single altar of sacrifice—even as also there is but one bishop."[21] This certainly is why Ignatius presents his impending martyrdom as his being ground into "a meal for the beasts"

<hr/>

[20]   *Letter to the Ephesians* §4; Staniforth, *op. cit.*, p. 62.
[21]   *Letter to the Philadelphians* §4; Staniforth, *op. cit.*, p. 94. At his *Letter to the Smyrnaeans* §8, an illuminating convergence occurs between the Eucharist, the monoepiscopacy, and the first-ever use of the term "Catholic": "The sole Eucharist you should consider valid is one that is celebrated by the bishop himself, or by some person authorized by

because he is "God's wheat, ground fine by the lions' teeth to be made purest bread for Christ."[22] This then becomes a central metaphor for the Christian life which we shall see in various ways throughout the early days of the Church, to become the Body of Christ for others, to become Christ for the world.

The visible unity of the Church parallels the unity of the Eucharist. Both are unified through a divine cohesion: just as the divine unites with the human in the person of Jesus Christ, that same divine life reaches communicants through the natural appearance of bread and wine, and the Church is a divine body whose works are run by mere men. To belong to Christ is to find oneself unified in his Church in both thought and action. If one discovers that he or she has fallen away, "repent and come back into the unity of the Church, they too shall belong to God, and so bring their lives into conformity with Jesus Christ. But make no mistake, my brothers; the adherents of a schismatic can never inherit the kingdom of God."[23] While not all second-century thinkers had this strong of an emphasis on episcopal authority and its intended unity, Ignatius displayed a robust concern for not only the intended communion between all Christians but also for an even deeper transformation of the Christian into Christ; thus did the Church's doctrine of the Mystical Body begin to take shape.

him. Where the bishop is to be seen, there let all the people be; just as wherever Jesus Christ is present, we have the Catholic Church," p. 103.
[22] *Letter to the Romans* §4; Staniforth, *op. cit.*, p. 86.
[23] *Letter to the Philadelphians* §3; Staniforth, *op. cit.*, p. 103.

Letter of Barnabas

Also considered among the writings of the Apostolic Fathers is the *Letter of Barnabas*, written shortly after these letters of Ignatius—mid to late second century (while some have argued for both earlier and later dates), with a composition date between 120 and 130 as a safe estimate. Here is an anonymous theologian trying to explain the Catholic faith by drawing mainly from the Old Testament. The *Letter of Barnabas* is not necessarily directed toward a Jewish audience, for by the first third of the second century, it is clear that Christians are a distinct cult and are not returning to the Temple and the ways of the Old Covenant. In fact, in many ways, Barnabas's interlocutor is quite anti-Jewish: the letter condemns God's people for not understanding their Messianic prophecies properly. This is the letter's central question concerning unity: How are Christians to approach and assimilate their reading and interpretation of the Hebrew Scriptures?

The author of *Barnabas* most likely knew there were some Christians leery of making Jesus Christ too human, too historical. Deemed now as heretical factions, some early Christians struggled to accept the fullness of Jesus's humanity as well as his Jewishness. For instance, one of the earliest heretical groups interacting with Christians came to be known as the Docetists (from the Greek *dokeo*, "to appear"). Docetists worshipped Jesus but taught that the Son of God only *appeared* to be human, only appeared to be a Jewish carpenter, surely something too lowly for God

to actually become.[24] To correct these misconceptions, the
author of *Barnabas* insists that the story of the Christ must
be rooted in history, in the promises Yahweh has made to
his people for millennia. Accordingly, Christ's story begins
in Israel; in fact, it even begins in Eden. The New Adam
shows that there are not two stories to God, not two promises. The Christ event assumes all other divine promises
into himself. The God represented in *Barnabas* is one of
humble love who is willing to do what is necessary to draw
others to himself, as seen in God's calling lowly herdsmen
like Abraham and through his using a panoply of patriarchs, prophets, judges, and unfaithful kings to accomplish
his purposes, culminating in God himself assuming lowly
flesh in the manger at Bethlehem.

The author of *Barnabas* bases his letter on the theme
of the "Two Ways" evident throughout the Old Testament:
there is life and there is death, there is light and there is
darkness, truth and fallacy, heaven and hell. To explain how
to discern these exclusively opposite ways of life, the writer
begins his letter by setting out how to read the Old Testament properly now in light of Christ's advent. The second
half of his letter is then dedicated to this "two ways" motif:
"Between these two Ways there is a vast difference, because

---

[24]   The Docetist sect is surely the group the Apostle John came to
know, and that is why the Johannine epistles stress so surely and fre-
quently the flesh of Christ; e.g., "That which was from the beginning,
which we have heard, which we have seen with our eyes, which we
have looked upon and touched with our hands, concerning the word
of life—the life was made manifest, and we saw it, and testify to it, and
proclaim to you the eternal life which was with the Father and was
made manifest to us" (1 Jn 1:1–2).

over the one are posted the light-bearing angels of God, and over the other the angels of Satan; and one of these two is the Lord from all eternity to all eternity, while the other stands paramount over this present age of iniquity."[25] This early letter attributed to the Apostle Barnabas, although his authorship is unlikely, is ultimately a treatise on spiritual discernment: how should one read Scripture and how, then, does one apply that living word to life in this world?

St. Polycarp (d. c. 160)

Another important bishop during this foundational time was Polycarp of Smyrna (c. 70–c. 160), who was also put to death for carefully protecting and teaching the Christian people entrusted to him. We know that Polycarp was the bishop of Smyrna (in today's Turkey) as Ignatius passed through in 107, consecrated *episcopus* (the Greek word for bishop is telling: *epi-*, the prefix for "over," and *scope*, meaning "to see") there by the Apostle John himself. Not much else is known of Polycarp, although we do have his letter to the Church at Philippi, a widely popular martyrial act from the second century, as well as his appearances in other early Church writings. Polycarp watched over his people by insisting on the fittingness and the beauty of the Son's becoming flesh against the Docetic tendencies of his age which reduced the body to a distraction and a scandal. From St. Irenaeus of Lyons, we know that Polycarp went to Rome toward the end of his life to ask Pope Anicetus (157–168) when the Church in Smyrna should celebrate

---

25   *The Epistle of Barnabas* §18; trans. Staniforth, *op. cit.*, p. 179.

Easter, again attesting to how the bishop of Rome exercised a universal authority for the sake of ecclesial unity from the earliest days of the Faith.

Polycarp's martyrdom provided much spiritual edification and inspiration for the early Church. One can see why when reading the following account:

> As Polycarp stepped into the arena there came a voice from heaven: "Be strong, Polycarp, and play the man!" . . . Finally he was brought before the Governor who asked if this was the man and when Polycarp admitted it, he tried to persuade him to recant. "Have some respect for your years," he said; adding the rest of the usual exhortation, "Swear an oath 'By the Luck of Caesar.' Own yourself in the wrong and say about your Christians, 'Down with the infidels!'" Polycarp's brow darkened and he threw a look around the turbulent crowd of heathens in the circus; and then, indicating them with a sweep of his hand, he said with a growl and a glance to heaven, "Down with the infidels!" The Governor, however, still went on pressing him. "Take the oath and I will let you go. . . . Revile your Christ." Polycarp's reply was, "Eighty and six years I have served him and he has done me no wrong. How then can I blaspheme my King and my Savior?"[26]

Well, the governor then had the funeral pyre lit and called out to the crowd that, in fact, Polycarp had admitted to being a Christian and acclaimed as a bishop, a representative

---

[26]   *The Martyrdom of Polycarp* §9; trans. Staniforth, *op. cit.*, p. 128.

of Jesus Christ on earth who alone is "the Savior of our souls, the Master of our bodies and the only Shepherd of the Catholic Church the wide world over."[27]

Typical of these early martyrologies, drama is mixed with dogma. We are brought into the suspense of a Christian's being captured and interrogated over his fidelity to this strange oriental messiah Jesus Christ. Refusing to place the Roman Caesar above or even equal to the one, true Lord, the martyr always faces some excruciating death, the description of which rarely fails to include gruesome details along with catechetical content. So, refusing to deny Christ, the aged bishop is sentenced to death, and the executioners place him unbound on the pyre. But then all of a sudden, without the assistance of any wind, "the fire took on the shape of a hollow chamber, like a ship's sail when the wind fills it, and formed a wall around the martyr's figure; and there he was in the centre of it, not like a human being in flames but like a loaf baking in the oven."[28] Readers are thus taught how the bishop is the overseer of the barque of Peter, symbolized by the sails of the ship; he is the one who is most visibly living out his vocation to become Christ's body. Death in Christ does not bring disfigurement or decay; it brings life and nourishment.

Here Polycarp is depicted as becoming bread, becoming Eucharist. In his imitation of Christ's own death, the bishop becomes *alter Christus*, "another Christ" continuing the Eucharist in the world by loving example and selfless service to his Church. Yet, since the flames did not disfigure

---

[27]   Ibid., §19; Staniforth, *op. cit.*, p. 131.
[28]   Ibid., §15; Staniforth, *op. cit.*, p. 130.

and refused to consume Polycarp, the Romans resorted to the daggers: "Finally when they realized that his body could not be destroyed by fire, the ruffians ordered one of the dagger-men to go up and stab him with his weapon. As he did so, there flew out a dove, together with such a copious rush of blood that the flames were extinguished."[29] *The Martyrdom of Polycarp* is a fine example of the early Church's building a "rule of faith," a guidebook advising which saints are worthy of emulation, whose theological terms and images can be trusted, and who can be invoked liturgically for prayerful intercession.

Bishop Papias of Hierapolis

An early bishop of Hierapolis, a small city in southwestern Turkey, named Papias (c. 70–c. 163) is often counted among the Apostolic Fathers. We have only fragments of his *Exposition of the Sayings of the Lord*, a sort of early commentary on the Gospels. But early on in this work, we read one of the first attestations to the process by which the books of the Bible came to be considered canonical. Such a recognition and subsequent selection of what "utterances" could be deemed divinely inspired were the third major issue the early Church had to clarify.

This fragment by Bishop Papias and the *Letter of Barnabas* each served to help early Christians read and understand the Bible correctly. These Christian writers represent an essential step in Christianity's development because at her beginning, the Catholic Church was not given a list

---

29   Ibid., §16; Staniforth, *op. cit.*, p. 130.

of books which should be considered divinely inspired and thus included in the Bible. One of the first questions in this process was: What does the Old Testament have to do with the New? After all, whereas the Gospels represent a God who is a healer and a speaker of truth always, the Hebrew writings tend to depict a God who incites war, uses deceptive ruses to get his way, and seems to approve of polygamy, and so on.

Questions like these were first posed to the Catholic Church by Marcion of Sinope (d. c. 160). Displaying the typical gnostic tendency to separate spirit from matter and heavenly truths from historical realities, Marcion consequently ripped the Old Testament away from the New. In Marcion's view, the Hebrew canon should not be included in the Christian proclamation. He also excised most of the Gospel stories that had to do with anything overly earthy regarding the now incarnate God and included only ten of the thirteen Pauline epistles found in today's New Testament. Marcion's aim was to denigrate the God of the Old Testament as an unworthy deity embedded in matter, the Jewish people as an unfaithful race, and Jesus Christ as a new revelation (of whom Marcion was the only true apostle, of course) who has come to condemn life in this world and all that being embodied entails.

As absurd as such a trajectory sounds to us today, who was there to tell Marcion he was wrong? The Bible did not come with a table of contents readily available; at this point in Christianity, there was no established theology of understanding how the Church should read the Old Testament in light of the New. To protect the integrity of the Faith, the

Lord raised up theologians and inspired Church councils to articulate how the Christian people can never separate God's first covenant from his final and definitive testament in Christ. Marcion's deprecation of matter and his inability to see how the events and figures of the Old Testament all foreshadowed an even greater one to come in the flesh, would be recognized then, and still is today, for the heresy which it is.

Scholars have uncovered a famous fragment, dating to the second century, containing the oldest list of canonical writings extant for what would eventually be named the New Testament. The so-called *Muratorian Fragment* includes approximately eighty-five lines of Latin text referring to Pope St. Pius I (140–157) but also to the Gnostic threats orthodox authors of this time knew, Basilides and Marcion. Named after the Italian scholar, Ludovico Muratori, who discovered this tiny fragment in the Library of St. Ambrose in Milan in 1740, this small bit of parchment includes as divinely inspired the four Gospels, all thirteen letters of St. Paul, the letters of Jude and of John, the book of Revelation, but also the Wisdom of Solomon, the Apocalypse of St. Peter, and even the *Shepherd of Hermas*, included as a book of "private devotion." Here we can see how the second century was a pivotal time in rushing to figure out what books should be considered divinely inspired and which could be relegated to popular devotion, helpful for private "spiritual reading" but not worthy of public and liturgical proclamation.

Shepherd of Hermas

We have already seen the popularity of the *Shepherd of Hermas*, the last liturgical book to be deemed non-canonical. Its pages originated in the second century (but were not finished until much later), and they extol the glorious mercy of Christ and his Church. This relatively lengthy work would be among the last removed from the local canons as biblically inspired and thus deemed to be profitable spiritual reading only. In all likelihood, this text arose in Rome to combat a certain rigorism which could not see how Church unity and grave or repeated sinfulness could coexist. Perhaps this thinking arose during some local persecution of Christians, but the Shepherd is insistent that the wellsprings of the sacrament of Reconciliation never dry up and there is always hope for those who wish to return to Christ. Even husbands whose wives have committed the sin of adultery are instructed to welcome their spouse back if she is at all repentant.

At one point in this story, the former slave known only as the Shepherd has a vision of a woman who is at once young and beautiful while also aged and advanced in years. Why so? She represents the Church who is always simultaneously new and countercultural, while also being ancient and everlasting. When asked why she appears old, the Church responds that she is older than the world because the world was created for her. We see how the Church today has relied on this ancient belief, and in the *Catechism of the Catholic Church*, we today read:

Christians of the first centuries said, "The world was created for the sake of the Church" (*Shepherd of Hermas*, Vision 2.4.1). God created the world for the sake of communion with his divine life, a communion brought about by the "convocation" of men in Christ, and this "convocation" is the Church. The Church is the goal of all things (Bishop Epiphanius, d. 403; *Panarion* 1.1), and God permitted such painful upheavals as the angels' fall and man's sin only as occasions and means for displaying all the power of his arm and the whole measure of the love he wanted to give the world: Just as God's will is creation and is called "the world," so his intention is the salvation of men, and it is called "the Church" (Clement of Alexandria, d. 215; *The Teacher*, 1.6).[30]

Fitting with a constant theme we have mentioned before, unity and charity in the Christian vision are coextensive. Christ's will for his people is a harmonious unity, a convocation, where community and concord reflect the perfect love of the Trinity as well as the gathering of otherwise separated grains and grapes to make up the bread and wine of Holy Communion.

This was how a Rule of Faith developed. Pious observances, turns-of-phrases, and technical terms which clarified some Christian mystery, along with the inspiring stories and legendary lives of holiness, were slowly built up and safely "deposited" under this continuing canon which filtered and formalized the living practice of the Faith.

---

[30] CCC §760.

Church leadership, liturgical practices, hagiographies, and martyrologies, all fall under this rubric.

In fact, the most conclusive list of inspired books which match the finalized version of the New Testament we have today did not appear until late in the fourth century, coming from a *Paschal Festal Letter* of St. Athanasius, bishop of Alexandria in Egypt. At most major feasts, Easter especially, a high-ranking bishop of a major see would advise his people on some important pastoral topic, fully aware that his letter would be transmitted throughout all the smaller dioceses in the vicinity. During Eastertide of 367, Athanasius devoted his paschal writings to the canonicity of Scripture and the importance of the right books being proclaimed liturgically so as to lead the people in holiness:

> But for greater exactness I add this also, writing of necessity; that there are other books besides these not indeed included in the Canon, but appointed by the Fathers to be read by those who newly join us, and who wish for instruction in the word of godliness. The *Wisdom of Solomon*, and the *Wisdom of Sirach*, and *Esther*, and *Judith*, and *Tobit*, and that which is called the *Teaching of the Apostles*, and the *Shepherd*. But the former, my brothers and sisters, are included in the Canon, the latter being merely read; nor is there in any place a mention of apocryphal writings. But they are an invention of heretics, who write them when they choose, bestowing upon them their approbation, and assigning to them a date, that so, using them as

ancient writings, they may find occasion to lead astray the simple.[31]

The question of which Old Testament books were canonical needlessly resurfaced in the sixteenth century when some of the Reformers questioned the canonicity of the Church's Old Testament of forty-six books.[32] This tampering forced the Church Fathers at the Council of Trent (1545–63) to declare the canon closed and anathematize anyone who would dare question the inspiration of the seventy-three books of the Bible of the ancient Church (confirming the fourth-century Council of Carthage in Trent's document, *De Canonicis Scripturis*). In tracing this history, we can now see how today's versions of the Holy Bible really are the result of God incessantly guiding his Church to come to embrace his will through centuries of the Church's own prayerful study and discernment. Through his apostles, saints, sanctioned synods, and councils, the Lord himself never fails to provide truth and direction for his people.

We have now seen that the most pressing issues the early Church had to clarify in order to solidify ecclesial unity were, first, proper leadership structure—i.e., one bishop presiding over a given geographical area—which would gradually lead to the formation of dioceses and archdioceses, and metropolitan sees, with the bishop of Rome overseeing

---

[31] Athanasius, *Festal Letter* 39.7; trans. Archibald Robertson, *Nicene and Post-Nicene Fathers*, vol. 4, *op. cit.*, p. 552.

[32] These original forty-six canonical books of course differ from the thirty-nine books accepted as divinely inspired by Luther and others, giving rise to the Protestant "apocrypha," those seven books received as truly biblical by Catholics.

all universal decisions affecting the one Church. The second issue was the development of a set way of Christian life, what came to be known generically as the living Rule of Faith, the *regula* in Latin or the *kanon* in Greek—the measuring stick or gauge of truth. The third issue was the definitive choice regarding which books should be considered as part of the Bible, and which would be declared false or erroneous or, if not inspired, which could be edifying for the faithful to read simply for private devotion, edification, and prayer.

As important and as essential as those declared to be doctrinal texts were in the early Church, they were not the most widely read documents at this time. That distinction belongs to the first martyrial acts we have: the martyrdoms of Clement, Ignatius and Polycarp, the story of the Scillitan martyrs of 180 (the first Christian text we have originally composed in Latin), and even later accounts offering adventure as well as solid teaching. These were the day's "top sellers" because they each revealed how the early Christians came to embrace the cross living under an intolerant and fear-filled Roman government. There is solid theology in these martyrial recordings, but there is also an aspect of spiritual entertainment.

As long as Rome could count on all of its citizens to pray to the right gods and goddesses at the proper time during the year, during the time of war and civic need, each citizen could also include any deity he wanted in his own private devotions. What Rome could not tolerate were those who refused to bow to its great pantheon. In fact, while poorer Romans had ceramic images, the wealthier used all sorts of silver and gold to represent their favorite household gods (*di penates*), and it was well known that Emperor Alexander Severus (222–35) had set up in his inner-atrium statues of Abraham, Orpheus, and Jesus Christ, hardly distinguishing between them. As such, Christ himself was not a threat to Rome. The threat was the exclusivity of the Christian claim and a rapidly-increasing demographic who worshipped this man as God and no one else (cf., Acts 4:12). Such exclusivity and its expansion were of course noticed; something novel was clearly afoot, and Rome sought to stamp out what they perceived to be a dangerous new superstition.

Persecutions: A Brief History of Early Christian Martyrdom

One of the first reports of Christian persecutions comes not from their losing some noble debate, from being intellectually misunderstood or ridiculed for some fanciful doctrine. They were scapegoated for the mistake of a madman. The historian Tacitus (d. 117) recalls an infamous story of how the Emperor Nero (54–68) used a supposed brewing hatred of Christians to dispel the rumors that the emperor himself had been guilty of widespread arson: "To allay the scandal or banish the belief that the fire had been ordered . . . Nero set up as the culprits and punished with the utmost refinement of cruelty a class hated . . . who are commonly called Christians. *Christus*, from whom their name is derived, was executed at the hands of the procurator Pontius Pilate in the reign of Tiberius. . . . Accordingly, arrest was first made of those who confessed [sc. to being Christians]; then, on their evidence, an immense multitude was convicted, not so much on the charge of arson as because of hatred of the human race."[33]

Nero drew on the populace's disregard and obvious suspicion of those who did not worship the way they did. Rome knew what happened to Christ decades earlier just outside of Jerusalem. Roman historians knew that from this name a new people had made their way to Rome and beyond. It was this novelty that the old Romans would exploit, translating their worship of Christ into hatred for Rome and its ancient ways. Tacitus thus continues:

> Besides being put to death they were made to serve as objects of amusement; they were clad in the hides of beasts and torn to death by dogs; others were crucified, others set on fire to serve to illuminate the night when daylight failed. Nero had thrown open his grounds for the display, and was putting on a show in the circus, where he mingled with the people in the dress of a charioteer. . . . All this gave rise to a feeling of pity . . . for it was felt that the Christians were being destroyed not for the public good but to gratify the cruelty of an individual.[34]

Why were the Christians accused of hatred, the very thing that Christ forbade most explicitly by so clearly commanding his followers to love all? In a society where the public weal as well as all the public woes were considered the direct result of the gods' and goddesses' blessings (and curses), if

---

[33]   Tacitus, *Annals* in *Documents of the Christian Church*, ed. Henry Bettenson (Oxford University Press, 2nd ed., 1963), p. 1-2.
[34]   Ibid.

a faction of that population would not invoke the deities of the state, that meant that they were not participating fully in that which brought bounty to Roman towns and to Latin farms. The Christians were thus first accused of "hating the human race" because the Romans saw how they did not pray rightly, did not rely on the emperor and his cult, his worship, for their well-being.

For example, from the late first century, we have a coin from the reign of Domitian (81–96). The emperor himself would have had this coin minted, etched, and invoked as the *Dominus et Deus*, the Lord and the God of all peoples under him. That is why the Roman Christians could not acknowledge the emperor in the same way as the other Romans; this is why they were accused of hating society. For in refusing to worship the deities of Rome, the Christians were perceived as unpatriotic to those around them. It was thus not for theological reasons the Christians were persecuted. Like most ancient Mediterranean religions, Rome always had room for one more deity, and certainly would have allowed Jesus's followers to have worshipped him as one wonder-worker among many. But Catholics became enemies of the state not because they worshipped Christ; they were persecuted for *not* worshipping the gods and goddesses of Rome, for not offering sacrifice to the emperor who was a divinely appointed theocrat worthy of adoration. They may not have understood why Jesus was the Lord, why the cross was ultimately a sign of victory, but they certainly could have made room for such a God in their pantheon if the first Christians would have allowed them to do so. But today's Christian ancestors were rightly very stubborn, very stiff-necked: Christ alone is God and he alone is to be worshipped, and for this those first disciples knew they would undergo persecution. "Yet if one suffers as a Christian, let him not be ashamed, but under that name let him glorify God" (1 Pt 4:16).

Since Roman religion was civic in nature, part of their worship was to offer sacrifices to the emperor if one lived in Rome, or to the emperor's image in mosaic if one lived away from the capitol. In a letter dated around 112, we hear Pliny the Younger, a Roman philosopher and legal magistrate, write back to the emperor Trajan (98–117) from his outpost in Bithynia (a Roman Province in Asia Minor) informing him that "an anonymous pamphlet was issued, containing many names" of Christians. Pliny had those people called in, and "all who denied that they were or had been Christians I considered should be discharged, because they called upon the gods at my dictation and did reverence, with incense and wine, to your image which I had ordered to be brought forward for this purpose, together with the statues of the deities; and especially because they cursed Christ, a thing which, it is said, genuine Christians cannot be induced to do."[35]

The term "martyr" was originally a legal term, stemming from the Greek word meaning "witness." St. Stephen (Acts 6:8–8) was the first Christian reported to have been martyred by those who simply could not fathom Christ alone as God. Yet the early Church had a tradition in which Christ was the first martyr, the original one who came to earth to

---

[35] Pliny the Younger, *Epistle 10 to Trajan*; trans. Bettenson, *op. cit.*, p. 3.

witness to the power and love of God the Father. Also, in the early Church this pouring out of one's own lifeblood was seen as a form of baptism; we have reports of crowds of Christians attending these public martyrdoms yelling *salvum lotum, salvum lotum,* "saved and washed, saved and washed," seeing in the martyrs' blood a form of baptismal waters.

We saw earlier the martyrologies of Ignatius and of Polycarp, but the most popular story to be told was the ancient passion of two holy women, the North African martyrs Perpetua and Felicity. Perpetua was a young noble-woman and Felicity was her slave-girl, pregnant with a child. Both were condemned for being faithful Catholics in the year 202 or 203 when the emperor Septimus Severus ordered the recantation of all Christians. As they were led into the Circus in Carthage, there were pleas from all sides: from the Romans to enjoy a bloody spectacle, and from the family of Perpetua for her to recant and for Felicity to save her baby by doing the same. Two days before the contests, however, Felicity went into labor, and while delivering her child, one of the Roman prison guards snapped at her, "You suffer so much now—what will you do when you are tossed to the beasts?" At which Felicity retorted, "What I am suffering now, I suffer for myself. But then another will be inside me who will suffer for me, just as I shall be suffering for him."[36] Again, the Christ is born and suffers and is ultimately resurrected in the life of each of his believers.

---

[36] *Martyrial Act of Perpetual and Felicity* §15; trans. Herbert Musurillo, *The Acts of the Christian Martyrs* (Oxford: The Clarendon Press, 1972), pp. 124–25.

This is what gave these early martyrs the perseverance needed to continue in the fight. Or, as we read next, the unknown author of this story then tells about Perpetua's martyrdom:

> [She] took the trembling hand of the young gladiator and guided it to her throat. It was as though so great a woman, feared as she was by the unclean spirit, could not be dispatched unless she herself were willing.
>
> Ah, most valiant and blessed martyrs! Truly are you called and chosen for the glory of Christ Jesus our Lord! And any man who exalts, honors, and worships his glory should read for the consolation of the Church these new deeds of heroism which are no less significant than the tales of old. For these new manifestations of virtue will bear witness to one and the same Spirit who still operates, and to God the Father almighty, to his Son Jesus Christ our Lord, to whom is splendour and immeasurable power for all ages.[37]

Throughout this and other stories of the martyrs, we can hear the crowd yell *salvum lotum, salvum lotum*—"Saved and washed, saved and washed!" The blood of martyrdom effected the waters of baptism in these early contests against the powers of the world. Women and men who were chosen to witness so fiercely to the tenderness of Christ were thus held up as worthy not only of emulation but intercession as well, relics of the martyrs marking the first major spots of pilgrimage in the Christian world.

---

[37]   Ibid., §21; Musurillo, *op.cit.*, p. 131.

As dramatic as these early stories of Christian persecution are, we see that after a while it was no longer enough to merely be considered a Christian. The novelty of Christianity was wearing off, so as the Christians were proving to be faithful Roman citizens who too paid taxes and served in many civic capacities, the Roman aristocracy had to trump up the charges. They hence devised the most heinous crimes they could think of; namely, incest and cannibalism. This is how Eusebius of Caesarea can report: "Among those arrested were some of our heathen domestics, as the governor had publicly announced that we were all to be hunted out. These were ensnared by Satan, so that fearing the tortures which they saw inflicted on God's people, at the soldiers' instigation they falsely accused us of Thyestean banquets and Oedipean incest, and things we ought never to speak of or think about, or even believe that such things ever happened among human beings."[38]

Eusebius records how the propaganda against Christians sought to make their story known through the even better known tales from Greek mythology; namely, the stories of Thyestes and Oedipus. Thyestes and his twin brother Atreus were competing for the throne of Olympia when Atreus's wife, Aerope, fell in love with Thyestes and began an adulterous affair. In Greek tragedy, it is usually best not to cheat on one's brother with his wife, so when Atreus learned what was going on, he killed Thyestes's two sons and dismembered them. Back in the kitchen of his house, he saved the remaining body parts and invited his

---

[38]   Eusebius, *The History of the Church* 5.1; trans. Williamson, *op. cit.*, p. 141.

unfaithful wife, Aerope, along with his brother, Thyestes, to dinner. Atreus fed them both the stew made from the flesh of Thyestes's own two sons, even going so far as to taunt him mid-bite by revealing the bloody heads and hands.

While accusations of cannibalism seem ludicrous to us today, they point to a deeper truth. Since Christ's founding of his Church, Catholics have been accused of indulging in a type of "Thyestean banquet" because the Church has always understood her origin to be the very Body and Blood of the Lord Jesus Christ, born in Bethlehem and partaken at every Holy Communion. Ancient bishops knew the natural aversion some might have in consuming Christ's living flesh (only cannibals eat human flesh), and so we hear homilies explaining that just as Christ did not "look" like God, so he was; just as that holy Bread and Wine do not "look" like the Body and Blood of Jesus, so they are. One of the great early bishops in Jerusalem, Cyril (d. 386), preached to his flock on this subject: "Stop, therefore, considering the bread and wine to be ordinary; for they are body and blood according to the Lord who made the declaration. For even if your senses suggest this to you, let faith confirm you. Do not judge this by taste, but be informed without doubt from faith that you have been made worthy of the body and blood of Christ."[39] Such proclamations could easily be multiplied, but we see why Christians could be thought to be cannibals, ordered to drink the Master's blood and to consume his flesh (Jn 6:53), so as to have his own life within us.

---

[39] Cyril of Jerusalem, *Mystagogical Catecheses* 4.6 as in *Lectures on the Christian Sacraments*, trans. Maxwell E. Johnson (Yonkers, NY: St. Vladimir's Press 2017), p. 115.

Christianity had thus been labeled an "illegal religion" (*religio illicita*) for hundreds of years. Since early in its inception, it was an impermissible religion held in suspicion by those in power. At times, the government unleashed its power against Christianity, but not always and certainly not everywhere. For the most part, the Christians were tolerated, but every now and then they offered the empire an excuse to flex its muscle and try to prove to itself that the old ways of Rome were not passing. But by around the year 250, the empire is about 7 percent Catholic, and by the year 300, it will be well above 10 percent, but thereafter, the Church grew at an exponential rate. Just as significant was the fact that more and more converts were coming from the aristocratic echelons of high Roman society. The more learned, the more well-connected, the more wealthy folk, inlcuding many influential senators and soldiers, philosophers and procurators, came to Christ. The Church offered a God who could be known personally and interacted with as a loving friend; the Church witnessed to this love by making room for the poor and most vulnerable by honoring the divine image within them (the first hospitals in the Roman Empire were established by Christians in the fourth century), by protecting women against the patriarchy of Rome, and by providing a way of life that made one's life story purposeful and eternal.

While the Church was growing in the mid-third century, imperial Rome was in trouble. There were setbacks within the Roman government, multiple wars were stretching the military thin, and the empire was hit with some consecutive years of scarcity. In the year 249, shortly after his election, the emperor Decius ordered all within the empire to obtain certificates proving that they had offered prayers and sacrifices to him for divine blessings upon Rome. One of these certificates of sacrifice (a *libellus* in Latin, meaning "little book") was found in Egypt in 1893, an incredible testimony to what Roman citizens were subject to: "To the Commissioners for Sacrifices in the Village of Alexander's Island, from Aurelius Diogenes, son of Satabus, of the village of Alexander's Island, aged 72; scar on right eyebrow: 'I have always sacrificed to the gods, and now in your presence, in accordance with the terms of the edict, I have sacrificed and poured out libations and tasted the sacrifices, and I request you to certify to this effect. Farewell.' Dated this first year of the Emperor Caesar Gaius Messius Quintus Trajanus Decius (26 June 250)."[40] With this formal certification process, came the first ever empire-wide persecution of the Church, a persecution in which all Christian adults were systematically ordered to sacrifice to the gods and goddesses of Rome in every known major locale in the empire.

To say that the year 250 was rather eventful would be an understatement: Pope Fabian (236–50) was martyred in Rome, the theologian Origen died because of the cruel torture endured during this persecution, and the Roman priest Novatian began a separate church, setting himself up as a rival pope. As such, Novatian inaugurated a heretical tendency within the early Church we today call "rigorism" or the "Church of the pure," because he harshly maintained

---

[40] From *Documents of the Christian Church*, ed. Bettenson, *op. cit.*, p. 13, slightly adjusted.

that any Christian who succumbed during persecution should not, could not, be allowed back into the Church.

The good news is that rigorists like Novatian always lose. In this case it happened like this: after Pope Fabian was martyred, the Roman clergy elected Cornelius to the Chair of Peter (250–53), but Novatian, then an influential Roman presbyter, wanted a more strict and authoritarian leader and broke off from the Church. This "Novatian schism" was a short-lived split, but it signaled how the Church is truly more a hospital for sinners than a home for saints. Novatian himself was put to death under the Emperor Valerian either in 257 or 258, and some of his followers continued to break communion from the rest of the Church, but soon they either died off or were reconciled back.

Even the great bishop and saint of this time, Cyprian of Carthage (d. 258), had to be purified of some rigorism. The Decian persecutions were notably fierce in North Africa, and Cyprian for a time did not allow those who lapsed during the trials to be readmitted without being again baptized. This was in direct contradiction to the practice and instruction of the Church of Rome, and so Pope Stephen admonished Cyprian for his stance, and Cyprian recanted. Despite this tendency to be overly harsh with sinners, Cyprian wrote brilliantly on the need for Church unity and what to do with sinners who lapsed. For during his time, there were members of the Church who were not actually sacrificing but were instead simply purchasing certificates from the government stating that they had done so; they were, for example, family men only trying to avoid punishment. To such as these, as well as those who fell in actual deed by sacrificing or the priests who handed over the holy books or sacred vessels, Cyprian was quite strict. This rigorism on Cyprian's part led to a schism throughout the Diocese of Carthage where the persecutions were unusually severe and divisions ran deep.

A fruit of this renewed bloodshed and the widespread attacks on the Church was a new spirituality devoted to defending the Church as the Bride of Christ, the mother of all who bear Christ's name. Cyprian stands at the head of this movement, writing eloquently about the need to love the Church as one does one's own mother, the mother who gave birth to you, fed you, cared for you and instructed you, just as the Church does. Another North African theologian, Tertullian, described the Church as *domina mater ecclesia*, our matron and mother Church, while Origen of Alexandria highlighted her as the *sponsa Christi*, the bride of Christ, and Cyprian famously wrote in his treatise on the Church's unity that "you cannot have God for your Father if you have not the Church for your mother."[41] This type of devotion is something which the Roman worldview simply lacked: a relationship with a God who could be addressed and trusted intimately, a relationship in which this God providentially works for the good of all humanity in history. Christianity offered pagans of the ancient world a place for not only their intellects but their affections as well, as fostering a personal relationship with Christ opens

---

[41] St. Cyprian, *The Unity of the Catholic Church*, §6, as in *The Lapsed, The Unity of the Catholic Church*, trans. Maurice Bévenot, SJ (New York: The Newman Press, 1956), p. 49.

one's heart to the rest of the world. To this change, how-ever, the worldly grandeur that was Rome was not going to acquiesce easily.

In 284, a former army strongman and military leader was proclaimed emperor. Emperor Diocletian sought to suppress any religion out of step with classical Roman ide-als. In order to manage things better, he divided the empire into a western and an eastern half, with two capitols and two co-emperors. Diocletian aimed to return to Rome's golden age and therefore took on the title of *Augustus* and had his second-in-command, Maximian, hailed as *Caesar*. Diocletian and Maximian sought to rule the West with iron fists, and they turned first to non-Roman religions. They first outlawed popular Gnostic sects from the East, but by 303, they had turned their might against the Chris-tians. Looking back, we can now see that by the year 300, traditional Roman pagans probably sensed that Rome as they had known it was ending: it had relinquished much of its land to various groups in the east and in the north, its treasuries were nearly bankrupt, its armies strategically stretched and morally deflated, and even in the West there were attempts by those living in what are now France and Spain and Britain to secede from the empire and begin a "Gallic Empire." Rome clearly was in need of a new start, and in such times the pattern was to lash out at those who were not praying in the right temples to the right divinities.

On February 23, 303, Diocletian had the Catholic church in Nicomedia demolished, and he released his first *Edict Against the Christians* the following day, reinforcing laws against Christians gathering, owning property, and holding contraband bibles and books of prayer. By the month's end, a fire had broken out in the imperial palace across from where the destroyed church had just recently stood. Diocletian was convinced that this was an act of Christian conspiracy and responded inordinately and violently. He called for the universal imposition of sacrifices, the arresting of all Catholic bishops, priests, and deacons, and imposed cruel and savage penalties upon anyone for even assisting a Christian. These were the years of "The Great Persecution" lasting well after Diocletian's retirement (in 305), until Galerius finally rescinded his predecessor's anti-Christian *Edict* in 311. The empire teetered between an unlikely return to the past and a new acceptance of a group that was making converts and gaining influence. Politically astute and liberally minded in the best sense, Galerius thus allowed Christians to gather openly, reclaim any commandeered land and buildings, and pray as they saw fit. Once a passionate persecutor of Christians, Galerius saw the changes coming and in his dying days was reported to have issued this statement:

> After the publication of our edict, ordaining the Christians to betake themselves to the observance of the ancient institutions, many of them were subdued through the fear of danger, and moreover many of them were exposed to jeopardy; nevertheless, because great numbers still persist in their opinions, and because we have perceived that at present they neither pay reverence and due adoration to the gods, nor yet worship their own God, therefore we, from

our wonted clemency in bestowing pardon on all, have judged it fit to extend our indulgence to those men, and to permit them again to be Christians, and to establish the places of their religious assemblies; yet so as that they offend not against good order. . . . Wherefore it will be the duty of the Christians, in consequence of this our toleration, to pray to their God for our welfare, and for that of the public, and for their own; that the commonweal may continue safe in every quarter, and that they themselves may live securely in their habitations.[42]

There are not many naturally human reasons why, but through these many Christian martyrdoms, the empire began to awaken to the resilience of Christ's faithful. Through the violence of Decius in 250 and the universal pogroms under Diocletian in the early fourth century, the Christian God used the lives and deaths of his children to consecrate Rome. That is, from a small band of Jewish fishermen to this admitted "great number" of fervent followers of Christ, the Church began to change the culture.

We must, therefore, next turn to the first expressions of such a change, the writings of the original Christian Apologists. Through the Church's graced long-suffering and the application of the best of human wisdom to the riches of revelation, these Apologists began to show the people of Rome both the reasonableness of the Christian Faith as

---

[42]   Lactantius, *On the Deaths of the Persecutors* §34; trans. William Fletcher, *Ante-Nicene Fathers*, vol. 7, *op. cit,*, p. 314.

well as their injustice in persecuting those who were proving to be the empire's most faithful citizens.

Conclusion

Forced by persecution always to refine her thinking about
and expression of the truths of the Faith, the Church
came to produce a sizable body of literature aimed at both
explaining Christian truth as well as disproving pagan
claims against it. This body of literature emphasized three
keys to the recognition, articulation, and development of
true doctrine: (1) the authority of the bishop who symbolized authentic Christian unity, (2) the manner in which
Christians worshiped and prayed, and (3) the proper content and understanding of the Bible as informed by sacred
tradition. In other words, we understand earliest develop-
ments within Christianity by asking: (1) To whom must I
be obedient? Who is the one who represents Christ himself
here on earth and on what does he base his claim? (2) How
then am I to conduct myself as a worshipping and prayerful
follower of Christ? And (3) what books belong in the Bible
and how are they to be understood?

But now we have entered a new chapter, the age of the
Apologist. Between the age of the Apostolic Father and
the legalization of Christianity in 313 stood these brave
defenders of the Faith. Like those before and after them,
these writers too stressed the heart of Christianity as that
which sought union between Jesus and his followers. The
difference now was that this sacred Body was beaten and
bloodied, writing as they did during those decades when

Christian persecutions raged. Let us now examine the answers these comparatively peaceful Christians offered their mighty persecutors.

APOLOGY, ACCEPTANCE, AND THE COUNCIL OF NICAEA (325)

"My Father, who has given them to me, is greater than all, and no one is able to snatch them out of the Father's hand. I and the Father are one.' The Jews took up stones again to stone him. Jesus answered them, 'I have shown you many good works from the Father; for which of these do you stone me?' The Jews answered him, 'We stone you for no good work but for blasphemy; because you, being a man, make yourself God'" (Jn 10:29–33).

As WE HAVE seen, the Church's recognition that Jesus Christ and God the Father were one, and therefore no other God could be worshipped, brought bloody persecutions upon the Christian people. This non-negotiable unity between Jesus and his Father also brought internal upheaval as the Church fought to be true to both the monotheism blessedly inherited from their Jewish ancestors and the testimony of the Scriptures that this Jesus and his Father in heaven were obviously two different people but one nonetheless.

In our previous chapter, we examined the major persecutions of Christians by a Rome sensing its own mortal passing. After those tumultuous years of Christianity's exodus out of Jerusalem into the rest of the Mediterranean world, the next generation of Christian writers after the biblical authors have come to be known as the Apostolic Fathers, those who wrote from the late first to the late second century. As we saw, during these early years, Christianity was regarded as nothing more than an odd variation of traditional Judaism, but these men knew there was something wholly different with the inbreaking of the Messiah into human history. They accordingly went unnoticed by the worldly powers and focused their attention on Church leadership and organization, the ways Christians should fast and conduct themselves in the world, what they should read and understand as divinely inspired. In short, the Apostolic Fathers drew up the first Church manuals and Christian programs on how to grow in holiness.

But as the Church grew in number and in recognition, Rome in turn grew first suspicious and then outright hostile. Such a clash between a growing Church and an empire sensing its mortality gave rise not only to more widespread religious pogroms but also to a new form of Christian literature—the Apology. This became the formal way the early followers of Jesus could, as Pope Peter taught, "give an explanation" for the reason for the hope within them. The Christian apology set out to achieve a two-fold aim: to defend Christians against the outrageous denunciations leveled upon them by Rome and to show the Romans that their myths and traditions were self-contradictory and had secured a false "justice" for only a privileged few. The Christian creed and its insistence on loving conduct for all, especially the "least," on the other hand, showed how the fullness of truth and human dignity are not for only the learned and the leaders but for each and every human person.

This chapter will accordingly trace the major Apologists of the second and third centuries in order to show how the first generation of Catholic intellectuals used the power of the Gospel to defend Christianity from absurd interpretations, as well as how these writers sought to show Rome the error of its own story. While a chapter of this length cannot cover all the major figures of these formative centuries, we shall cover those most significant figures who demonstrated the unity of Christ and Christian in foundational ways. This chapter ends with a brief nod to the Apologists' hard-fought victory and the legalization of Christianity in 313. As we shall see, the emperor Constantine came not only to tolerate Christians as his predecessor Galerius desired but actually to legitimate, legalize, and even underwrite the Christian Church. What came to be known as the Edict of Milan (in 313) afforded Christians the same rights as other religious groups in the empire. This is not to imply that Constantine and his legalization of the Church either made Christianity known (it had been on the ascendancy for decades) or made it the official religion of the Roman Empire (which would in fact occur in 380 with Emperor Theodosius's promulgation of *Cunctos Populos*, known also as the Edict of Thessalonica). But, in granting the Christian people the same rights to worship publicly, own land and construct buildings, to gather legally, and to engage in open discourse with others, Constantine did provide the Church with an invaluable gift in allowing the fullness of her force and faith to be let loose on a culture in decay and searching for renewal. Among the more obvious fruits of the emperor Constantine's declaring the Catholic Church a *religio licita* was her ability to build public places, to worship freely, and to gather openly.

Second- and Third-Century Christian Apology

The term "apology" is derived from the Greek prefix *apo-*, meaning "apart" or "away from," and *logos*, meaning "reason" or, more simply, "word." An apology is, therefore, the use of words and reason to distance oneself from a false accusation or crime of illegal intent. In this sense, it has nothing to do with contrition or sorrow, as if making an apology for some harm done. In fact, it is almost the exact opposite: a position that I have been wronged and for those willing to listen, I shall make an apology, a defense, of what I actually hold and why this is in fact a reasonable position for all to hold as well. Plato's paean to his teacher Socrates, *The Apology*, gave this term the technical meaning it has enjoyed ever since. Sentenced to death in 399 BC for charges of impiety and corrupting the youth of Athens, Socrates was forced to drink hemlock and so publicly admit his guilt. Centuries later, St. John Henry Newman (1801–90) also composed an apology defending his decision to leave the highly stylized Church of England to enter the ancient Church of Rome. In his *Apologia Pro Vita Sua*, Cardinal Newman argues that while the Oxford Movement helped King Henry VIII's breakoff from Rome recover some of the liturgical beauty and ascetical practices which any serious Christian needs in this world, through prayer and study he knew he had to return to the Church that Christ himself founded.

Defense of one's beliefs against those who may not understand your reasons, or if they do, just disagree with you, has always been part of philosophical and religious odysseys. Early Christians were no different, and they wrote to answer the questions brought about when the Church was recognized as having finally broken away from the Temple in Jerusalem. Both Gentiles and Jews wondered who these new upstarts were: What did these Christians believe, and what were they going to bring into cities and communities? These were some of the questions for which the Christian had to provide a defense. This defense had to be made on two fronts and had two related goals.

The Christians had to engage the Jewish intellectuals on the one hand and the Roman philosophers on the other. First, against the learned Jewish scholars of the day, Christian writers presented life in Christ as both the final fulfillment of all the events God began with and through his first chosen people, but these fulfillments were also new invitations to follow God in a radical and more personal way. A vexing question thus arose: what now was the purpose of the old Law which Jesus Christ had fulfilled? What about all the Jewish customs and rituals these first Christians, converts from Judaism, would have not only known but in which they would have found great consolation most of their lives up to this point? With the Greek and Roman interlocutor, the questions to be answered were less cultic and more philosophical. Whereas the Jew and the Christian shared a common holy book and the same prophecies of the Hebrew people, the Gentiles of the Mediterranean world and the Christians shared a common humanity only, albeit a humanity in search of the same happiness and fulfilment which every human heart desires. That is why the questions which brought the Catholic and the pagan mind together revolved around the nature of God, the possibility and purpose of the Incarnation, and what exactly constitutes the good life.

If these were the two fronts on which early Christian apologetic was contesting, the two goals were just as clear. The first and immediate goal was to try to end the bloody persecutions of Christ's Body. The second was cleaner but just as important: to clarify doctrine and to show the reasonableness, the consistency, and the integrity of Christian doctrine and way of life. Where some of the Church's members went willingly to the arena, these theologians turned to their desks. Where some spilled their blood, these spilled their ink.

Quadratus of Athens (d. 129)

Not much else is known about this Greek theologian apart from the following fragment which appears in the historian Eusebius of Caesarea's (263–339) unmatchable history of the first three centuries of Christianity. Proceeding chronologically, Eusebius's *Ecclesiastical History* covers from the deaths of the apostles up to the year 324. It is an invaluable source of otherwise lost accounts of intrigue and Christian history. Listed as the first official apologist of the Faith is Quadratus of Athens, unfortunately without any introduction or biographical assistance. Eusebius simply relates:

> When Trajan had ruled for six months short of twenty years Aelius Hadrianus succeeded to the throne. To him Quadratus addressed and sent a pamphlet which he had composed in defence of our religion, because unscrupulous persons were trying to get our people into trouble. Many of the brethren still possess copies of this little work; indeed, I have one myself. In it can be found shining proofs of the author's intellectual grasp and apostolic correctness. He reveals his very early date by the wording of his composition.
>
> Our Saviour's works were always there to see, for they were true – the people who had been cured and those raised from the dead, who had not merely been seen at the moment when they were cured or raised, but were always there to see, not only when the Saviour was among us, but for a long time after His departure; in fact some of them survived right up to my own time.[43]

Quadratus wrote to Emperor Hadrian who ruled from 117–138 and was known to have continued Trajan's precedent that Christians should not be explicitly sought out. While never doubting that the Catholic Church constituted a *religio illicita*, Hadrian did insist only cases involving serious proof against Christians be heard.

---

[43]   Eusebius, *The History of the Church* 4.3; trans. Williamson, *op. cit.*, p. 106.

As Eusebius here highlights, Quadratus appealed to the resurrection of Jesus to show the emperor that this Christian faith was undeterred by death and would therefore prove to be an everlasting way of life. This is a common enough move for any Apologist of the second century: the works of Christ, the miracles, and ultimately his resurrection from the dead is what gave the early Christians their identity. As traversing through the Red Sea transformed an enslaved Hebrew people into the chosen Israelites, the Resurrection is the lens through which we read Church history. For if it were not for the Resurrection, there would be no New Covenant, no Catholic Church.

Aristides of Athens (d. 134)

If Quadratus is known to be the first Christian apologist, Aristides's treatise to the emperor Hadrian stands as the earliest preserved Christian apology. In fact, the next line in Eusebius's *Ecclesiastical History* reads, "Aristides again, a loyal and devoted Christian, has like Quadratus left us a *Defence of the Faith* addressed to Hadrian. Many people still preserve copies of his work also."[44] While Eusebius's Greek version of Aristides's *Apologia* places it squarely within Hadrian's rule (117–38), the Syriac edition says it was addressed to the emperor Antonius Pius (138–61), but we have now only fragments of both. Patching these fragments back together as well as possible, the reader is struck by Aristides's calm argumentation, going through the whole of human history and arguing how cultures become more and

---

44   Ibid.

more refined as they draw nearer to the one true God. This makes the Jews the most advanced of all the pre-Christian nations, but in the Church of Christ, humanity is finally offered its fullness.

Aristides takes the emperor Hadrian through his own version of world history, basing his comments off the four major races of humans: "Barbarians and Greeks, Jews and Christians." He catalogs each group and shows why Christianity is the perfection of what it means to be human. Whereas the Barbarians were duped into thinking of creatures as gods and goddesses, at least the Greeks sought the life of the mind and unchanging truth. The Jewish people were more advanced in their trust in the one true God and in their keeping of a higher moral code. Yet the Christians also keep the commandments but they exhibit a more universal charity because only followers of Jesus can live a divine life on earth, taking in strangers, calling all the baptized brother or sister without distinction of class or culture, fasting themselves so even the stranger has enough food for him and his family, and praying for all the dead, that all may be saved.[45] Such a superhuman life is possible because only the Christians live with God in their flesh, in their midst: "For great indeed, and wonderful is their doctrine to him who will search into it and reflect upon it. And verily, this is a new people, and there is something divine (lit: a divine admixture) in the midst of them."[46]

---

[45]   Cf., *Apology of Aristides* §16.

[46]   Ibid., trans. and ed. Allan Menzies, *Ante-Nicene Fathers*, vol. 9 (Hendrickson Publishers, [1896] 2004), p. 278.

Justin Martyr (d. 165)

Among the first to lay his life down for his literary output and not for a public act of imperial defiance is Justin, known since the second century as "the Martyr." (A student once asked me in class if he wasn't scared going through life known as "Justin the Martyr!" I gently let her know that he received this title only after his death.) One of the first respondents to the Roman accusations of infidelity and hedonism, Justin was a Greek philosopher turned Christian. He tells us his own life's story in his *Dialogue with Trypho*. Here in his intellectual quest to know the reality of things, Justin met an old, wise Jewish man who had just fled Israel because of the disturbances brought about by the Roman presence there. In their discussion, Trypho (most likely a fictional interlocutor) skillfully critiques central Christian claims by using the Hebrew Scriptures, while Justin counters by showing him that the truth all human persons seek is not a proposition but a Person. Throughout the rest of the exchange, Justin concerns himself mainly with showing Trypho that Christianity is the fulfillment of Judaism and that Christ's life and actions show that the prophecies of the Old Testament have now come true, clearly pointing to this Jesus as the Messiah.

Justin eventually moved to Rome to open a school. There he took on students and served as a sort of catechist for those who wished to know more about the Catholic faith, but in time, he had to defend his work (and his worship) and composed two *Apologiae*. These Apologies exhibit a high level of learning, Justin being steeped in Platonic as well as Stoic philosophy. He knew the Greek philosophical tradition well but also saw some major shortcomings to how Plato and others conceived of God and the good life. Justin's great contribution to Christian thought was to develop fully the significance of the Gospel of John's Prologue and the Evangelist's describing Christ as the eternal Logos. In stressing the Son of God as the eternal Logos—a technical term which we have already understood as "word," "reason," "rationale," and so on—Jesus Christ is hence revealed as the divine person who illumined all truth and logic. That is, it really is the Son of God who empowered the great Jewish patriarchs, inspired their prophets, and even granted wisdom to the Greek philosophers in their search to know the truth.

In other words, it was ultimately the Christ who inspired Moses, who gave Socrates his great insights, and so on. In turn, Justin tried to convince non-Christian thinkers that the reason and beauty they sought was the eternal Logos referenced in the Prologue of the Gospel of John. "In the beginning was the Word (Logos) and the Word (Logos) was with God and the Word (Logos) was God" (Jn 1:1). In this way, every truth, every act of virtue, every instance of magnificence is ultimately an encounter with the Son of God. But in choosing to call the Son Logos, John tapped into the philosophical world of the Greek mind, equating the one who will become Jesus Christ in the womb of Mary with truth, beauty, excellence, and purpose—the "logic" of all that is. Accordingly, when these are pursued, one pursues God. But human intelligence alone can never secure God, so God must come to us and elevate our lowliness and enlighten our ignorance. This is the entire purpose of the Incarnation; Justin tries to win the pre-Christian mind by telling those still outside the Church that:

> We have been taught that Christ First-begotten of God [the Father] and we have indicated above that He is the Word (Logos) of whom all mankind partakes. Those who lived by reason (Logos) are Christians, even though they have been considered atheists: such as, among the Greeks, Socrates, Heraclitus, and others like them; and among the foreigners, Abraham, Elias, Ananias, Azarias, Misael (cf., Dan 1:7; 3:20-93).... So, also, they who lived before Christ and did not live by reason were useless men, enemies of Christ, and murderers of those who did live by reason. But those who have lived reasonably, and still do, are Christians, and are fearless and untroubled.[47]

This is an amazing confession for someone who will soon meet the executioner's ax: all who seek truth truly are already Christians, despite whatever history may call them. While the Son of God may have come relatively late in time, Justin suggests, his power and influence were never absent from the rational soul. All who sought beauty and truth thus sought the Lord; all who found wisdom and virtue did so because the Son of God, the Logos, had welcomed them into his eternal life and the love of the Father.

---

[47] *First Apology* §46, as in St. Justin Martyr, *The First and Second Apologies*, trans. Leslie Barnard, *Ancient Christian Writers* (New York: Paulist Press, 1997), pp. 83–84.

Here we find the basis of the early Christians' use of myth and pagan wisdom. Since poets and philosophers like Homer and Plato, and patriarchs like Abraham and Moses, had correctly taught so many truths about the divine, about human nature, about the soul and the cosmos, those truths must have come from Truth himself. Christians, therefore, need not fear any culture which seeks to live rightly, regardless where it is found or under what form it is communicated. Truth never contradicts truth because the Logos, the Son of God, is its only true source and end. It is an amazing testimony to Christian virtue that a man living in a hostile territory who would soon be beheaded for his writings could tell his persecutors and those whom they emulate that if they live in accord with reason (Logos) they already are Christians.

Of course, Justin also knew that in the fullness of time, the Logos did come into the world, and this momentous event changed everything. Truth was now an enfleshed man who called all into himself through his Church, and into his Church through the sacraments entrusted to his priests now spread throughout all the world. Truly now the invisible has become visible. This is how Justin could write of the Eucharist around the year 150 in the following way:

> We call this food the Eucharist, of which only he can partake who has acknowledged the truth of our teachings. . . . Not as ordinary bread or as ordinary drink do we partake of them, but just as, through the word of God, our Savior Jesus Christ became Incarnate and took upon Himself flesh and blood for our

salvation, so, we have been taught, the food which has been made the Eucharist by the prayer of His word, and which nourishes our flesh and blood by assimilation, is both the flesh and blood of that Jesus who was made flesh.[48]

The word "transmutation" which Justin uses to describe how the bread and wine become the body and blood of Christ is the Greek equivalent of the Latin "transubstantiation," so we again see how unified, how organic, and how consistent Catholic theology is, and was even in its earliest days.

For Justin, the Logos, Wisdom, is no longer content with directing his followers from afar; he wants to enter into them and become as much one with them so as to be part of their own flesh and blood; it is for this reason that the Logos has become leaven, the Son of God has become the Bread of Life. For his success in promoting this truth of God's Body and Blood, Justin too would follow the martyr's path, shedding his own blood for defending the Faith against irrational hatred and unjust accusations.

Tatian (d. c. 180)

Not much is known of Justin's best known disciple, Tatian. What he is known for is called the *Diatesseron* (literally, "of four factors"), a very early attempt to reconcile all four Gospel stories into a seamless harmony. Whereas Matthew might stress a scene or a teaching from Jesus that, say, Luke and Mark did not, or when John includes a story that the

---

[48]   *First Apology* §66; trans. Barnard, *op. cit.*, pp. 105–6.

Synoptics fail to mention, Tatian has stitched these scenes together to provide a very lengthy account of Jesus's earthly life from the Annunciation to the Ascension by bringing all four Gospels together into a unified narrative. Tatian, we know, became Justin's student after meeting him in Rome around 160. After the death of Justin, not much is known about Tatian, although legends are consistent in relaying the unfortunate fact that Tatian either founded or freely joined a rigorous Christian sect known as the Encratites (Greek for "self-mastered"), severely stressing the ugliness of matter and the need to live a life apart from marriage and any sort of indulgence. It is a mark of intellectual charity to realize at this point in the life of Christ's Mystical Body that as topics were being debated and doctrines were being discerned, and a fuller explication of the truth was being sought, sometimes theologians—especially the more speculative—found themselves committed to thoughts or to communities which only later proved heretical or schismatic.

Epistle to Diognetus

Not much evidence is available to help contextualize this anonymously written letter to a man named Diognetus. The *Epistle to Diognetus* was certainly written during a time of Christian persecution, and given its early dating of 130 or so, it is sometimes included in the works of the Apostolic Fathers, but clearly its polemic tone and practical aims belong to the age of the Apologists. Here a sympathetic and educated pagan named Diognetus is curious about the

Catholic faith and asks for more insight into basic philosophical and theological questions. The letter, therefore, begins by refuting pagan idolatry and the nonsensical nature of polytheism. How can there be more than one Ultimate? The truth is that all of history originates and passes through the Jewish prophets and culminates in the one Logos whose redemptive suffering and myriad promises of resurrection usher in a new era in the ongoing history of humanity. This new Kingdom of God is already among us, realized by the growth of this same Christ's Church and evidenced by the integrity of her members.

Divided into twelve brief chapters (although chapters 11 and 12 are clearly later additions), the *Epistle to Diognetus* wants to make two basic claims. The first is that the life and nature of a human person is analogous to that of divine persons. Despite Roman tradition, a true God is not an unliving stone or a lowly creature (however precious) like silver or gold. This is why the author makes the point that there is no inherent difference between the stones that are prayed to and the ones on which we walk; there is no essential difference between the metals Romans sacrifice and the metals relied upon daily in everyone's kitchen and on everyone's farm. People are different, however, and that is why we all expect to be treated better than these subhuman existents, because we are God's images on earth.

This is why we are to act differently on earth, because we are no mere and finite beings who come into existence and decay out of being. This is the author's second main point. Human persons are not merely conglomerates of carbon but are in fact eternal children of a heavenly Father.

Christians alone understand that this world is the ante-chamber to heaven and that is why they live differently here, not getting caught up in the idolization of mere creatures but instead sojourn through these passing goods with an understanding that they have been given life eternal in Christ. This is perhaps the most memorable section of all the epistle's lines:

> To put it briefly, the relation of Christians to the world is that of a soul to a body. As the soul is diffused through every part of the body, so are Christians through all the cities of the world. The soul, too, inhabits the body, while at the same time forming no part of it; and the Christians inhabit the world, but they are not part of the world. The soul, invisible herself, is contained within a visible body; so Christians can be recognized in the world, but their Christianity itself remains hidden from the eye.
>
> The flesh hates the soul, and wars against her without any provocation, because she is an obstacle to its own self-indulgence; and the world similarly hates the Christians without provocation, because they are opposed to its pleasures. All the same, the soul loves the flesh and all its members, despite their hatred for her, and Christians, too, love those who hate them. The soul, shut up inside the body, nevertheless holds the body together; and though they are confined within the world as in a dungeon, it is Christians who hold the world together. The soul, which is immortal, must dwell in a mortal tabernacle; and Christians, as

> they sojourn for a while in the midst of corruptibility
> here, look for incorruptibility in the heavens.[49]

This beautifully crafted passage provides many insights
into the ancient apologetic: Christians suffer persecution
because this earth is not their home. This does not mean
that they are rootless and feckless tramps, but in fact they
preserve the world and elevate others by showing them that
unfading incorruptibility is possible in Christ. Neither does
this mean Christians are to live their lives on earth dour
and sullen; they enjoy the goods of this world as anyone is
entitled. Yet they do so with a constant gratitude expressed
through virtuous moderation and with an eye toward the
giver of all good gifts. Christians are unified in love of their
enemies and are therefore able to endure hatred in return
because they know to whom they truly and eternally belong.

Theophilus of Antioch (d. c. 183)

Tradition holds St. Peter as the first bishop of Antioch.
When he left Jerusalem, he went first up to modern-day
Syria to establish a Christian community and then left
for Rome, where he was arrested and eventually crucified
upside down. Accordingly, Antioch has always enjoyed a
certain primacy among the dioceses of the East, evidenced
by the careful cataloging of bishops (second in accuracy
only to Rome). Listed as the seventh bishop of this important bustling city is a certain Theophilus, recorded as holding
the episcopal see there from 169 to 183 (although some

---

[49]   *Epistle to Diognetus* §6; trans. Staniforth, *op. cit.*, p. 145.

lists date his death at 185). He fit the biographical pattern we have seen thus far: he was yet another learned Greek who had come to see the reasonableness and allure of the Christian creed, left his worldly career, and offered his intellect and his life to Christ and his Church. Unlike previous teachers, Theophilus was ordained into the priesthood and eventually became the *episcopus* of Antioch, in that city where Christians were first called Catholic by Ignatius generations earlier.

At one point in his Christian service, Theophilus was approached by a seeker named Autolycus who inquired into the nature of the Christian faith and how best to understand the nature of God and how the Christian God brought all of creation out of nothing. In his response, Theophilus broke new ground. He is the first Christian to comment on the opening of Genesis, and he is the first to use a technical term to describe the nature of the Triune God: "In like manner also the three days which were before the luminaries, are types of the Trinity, of God, and His Word, and His wisdom."[50]

In creating us in his own image and likeness, God did not create us for death, Theophilus explains, but we sadly chose it for ourselves. God created us with that great gift of free will, hoping for our affection and whole-hearted love, but he also allowed us to choose the nothingness from which he created us. As such, our lives teeter between the fullness of all reality and the emptiness which sin sadly brings about:

---

[50]   Theophilus of Antioch, *To Autolycus* 2.15; trans. B. P. Pratten, *Ante-Nicene Fathers*, vol. 2, pp. 100–1.

Was man made by nature mortal? Certainly not. Was he, then, immortal? Neither do we affirm this. But one will say, Was he, then, nothing? Not even this hits the mark. He was by nature neither mortal nor immortal. For if He had made him immortal from the beginning, He would have made him God. Again, if He had made him mortal, God would seem to be the cause of his death. Neither, then, immortal nor yet mortal did He make him, but, as we have said above, capable of both; so that if he should incline to the things of immortality, keeping the commandment of God, he should receive as reward from Him immortality, and [man] should become God.[51]

Theophilus captures a beautiful Christian insight here: while a god cannot be created by God, God can make "gods," and that is precisely what the Incarnation aims to achieve. From our emptiness, the Son of God empties himself so as to fill our brokenness with his own divine life. The Mystical Body and deification begin to coalesce in the thinking of the Apologists who want to stress how this beleaguered and persecuted Body can endure all things because we were never made solely for this world in the first place. Our true home is in heaven, our true life is as divinely adopted children of God.

Divided into three books, the *Ad Autolycum* is typical of the move we see from the Apostolic Fathers to the second-century Apologists: more theological sophistication, a

51 Theophilus of Antioch. *To Autolycus* 2:27; trans. Pratten, *Ante-Nicene Fathers, op. cit.,* p. 105.

defense of the Faith for the uninitiated who want to know more (as opposed to intramural Church manuals), and a still nascent explanation of the central Christian mysteries of the Trinity and the Incarnation. The Apologists wrote not to systematize the Faith but to present it to an outsider in a way that was reasonable. In these defenses, therefore, good theology and foundational premises are found but not at the level one will find in later Apologists and not, certainly, that found in the great Church Fathers who would have the space and leisure to think, pray, and write after the legalization of Christianity.

Athenagoras of Athens (d. 190)

At the end of the second century, two more apologies appear: the *Plea on Behalf of Christians* and the more popular *On the Resurrection of the Dead*. Both of these have the name "Athenagoras the Philosopher" attached to them, but this is about all we know of this Athenian academic turned Christian apologist. Both of Athenagoras's extant works explain some of the more countercultural aspects of the Christian faith: that Love is stronger than death, that the body is good and worth resurrecting into eternal life, and that Christians do not participate in cannibalism and incest as some outside the Church have rumored. These defamations are inconsistent with the virtue and the joy that Christians exhibit.[52]

---

[52] Among the more descriptive (and disturbing) accusations from around this time, as we have seen, is the claim that Christians ate the young and engaged in incestuous relations. The first accusation picks up, of course, on the Real Presence and the Christian's consuming

The *Plea on Behalf of Christians* was addressed to Marcus Aurelius (d. 180) and his court, displaying a respectful appreciation for this emperor's own philosophical astuteness. Athenagoras astutely appealed to the emperor's own love of Greek and Roman philosophy and knew that anyone this astute realized that there could be only one ultimate principle, only one ultimate cause of all that is. In fact, by this time of the Christian era, most pagan philosophers had concluded, along with the revelation of Jewish people, that there can be only one ultimate source of all that is. From this correct conclusion, Athenagoras goes on to mine the

---

Christ's Body and Blood; the second on the fact that Christian wives and husbands are first and foremost "brothers and sisters." The Latin Apologist Minucius Felix (d. c. 260) will later report: "An infant covered over with meal, that it may deceive the unwary, is placed before him who is to be stained with their rites: this infant is slain by the young pupil, who has been urged on as if to harmless blows on the surface of the meal, with dark and secret wounds. Thirstily — O horror!— they lick up its blood; eagerly they divide its limbs. By this victim they are pledged together; with this consciousness of wickedness they are covenanted to mutual silence. Such sacred rites as these are more foul than any sacrileges. And of their banqueting it is well known all men speak of it everywhere; even the speech of our Cirtensian testifies to it. On a solemn day they assemble at the feast, with all their children, sisters, mothers, people of every sex and of every age. There, after much feasting, when the fellowship has grown warm, and the fervour of incestuous lust has grown hot with drunkenness, a dog that has been tied to the chandelier is provoked, by throwing a small piece of offal beyond the length of a line by which he is bound, to rush and spring; and thus the conscious light being overturned and extinguished in the shameless darkness, the connections of abominable lust involve them in the uncertainty of fate. Although not all in fact, yet in consciousness all are alike incestuous, since by the desire of all of them everything is sought for which can happen in the act of each individual." Minucius Felix, *Octavius* §9; trans. Robert Ernest Wallis, *Ante-Nicene Fathers, op. cit.*, vol. 4, pp. 177–78.

classics of Greek philosophy and poetry to show that the good life as the Ancients have imagined it is what Christ not only models but what he alone can give. When honest, Athenagoras challenges his readers, the Greek mind must admit that no one, not even Socrates, has led this mortal life with integrity and selfless charity with a mind toward living forever in eternal joy, but Christians are now living on a higher plane with more integrity and charity than ever before. To live and die in perfect virtue and to thereafter live forever is what every human heart desires and in Christ, the Greeks learn, this new deified state is possible as not the contradiction to the truth they have sought for so long but as its perfect fulfilment.

From this concept, Athenagoras's treatise *On the Resurrection* (although some do doubt his authorship here, placing it a century or two later) follows: because Christians live on earth while actually dwelling (intellectually, spiritually, morally) as citizens of heaven, the resurrection is their eternal reward for living their temporal lives for Jesus Christ. The human person, Athenagoras clearly states, is neither a soul nor a body but an embodied soul, a spiritualized body, and the resurrection of the body is God's way of showing us rational creatures that we, as we are (body and soul), matter eternally. We again see that as the Christian faith left Jerusalem and made its way to Athens, it confirmed the truths that the Greek schools were working out (i.e., here, the goodness of matter and the need for body and soul to work together) as well as challenged where the Greek mind could not yet discover the fullness of reality (here, that this integrity between body and soul lasts forever in the final resurrection of all).

The central task of these early Apologists was not developing the doctrine of the Mystical Body, and so it appears only incidentally. As Christian theology unfolds through these decades, however, the unity between Christ and Christian receives a richer and more robust treatment. As the first becomes the second century, we meet one of the main exponents of this identification between divinity and humanity, a theologian known best for his theory of "recapitulation"; that is, the Son's making all things new in his divine descent. And so we now turn to one of the more sophisticated early Apologists, Irenaeus of Lyons.

Irenaeus of Lyons (d. after 191)

St. Irenaeus came from the Greek-speaking East, and as legend has it, he was made a bishop by Bishop Polycarp, whose martyrdom we recounted earlier. Irenaeus was then sent into Gaul (modern day France) to lead the growing Christian community there. Although we are not sure what became of Irenaeus at the end of his life, we know he was a most learned bishop of what is today Lyons, France, and most records hold him as a martyr, most likely during the great outbreak of persecutions under Septimus Severus (193–211) at the turn of the third century (the same persecutions which took the lives of the famed female martyrs Perpetua and Felicity in Carthage in 202).

That said, we do know that while Irenaeus was in Lyon, a place of rather sophisticated learning and intellectual curiosity, he encountered what we today call "Gnosticism," a word deriving from the Greek term for knowledge, *gnosis*. Dismayed by the various schools of Gnosticism, Irenaeus composed a lengthy work called *Against Heresies* in which he not only recalled the Gnostic leaders and systems of the late first and second centuries but also provided the Christian antidote to these wild systems of thought. What is Gnosticism? Although having emerged in various forms throughout history, it is always characterized by (what I refer to as) *the two D's*: dualism and deliverance.

In every Gnostic system, there are two opposing forces at war with one another. In this visible and temporal order, therefore, mutual hostility marks everything. Usually it begins with two deities: one good, the other malicious. At some point, these two gods come into contact with each other, resulting in a cosmos full of antagonistic opposites: light and dark, good and evil, war and peace, body and spirit, male and female, and so on. These systems must then provide some way to escape this world of warfare. Dualism is thus solved by deliverance, by a "secret sort of knowledge" that promises elite adherents some special way out of the "warring opposites" plaguing their very existence. They have to find a way out of their body, out of their sin, out of their darkness, out of their historical lives, their ageing, ongoing debilitations, and certain death. This is the stuff not only of second-century Gnosticism but it is precisely what New Age philosophy teaches as well: All difference is oppression, and absolute truth cannot be found in this world, a very different view than that God has unified all reality into himself by divinity's assuming humanity, the Creator becoming a creature, in Christ.

Many second-century Gnostics attempted to reconcile their tenets with the basic truths of Christianity. Take a fellow named Marcion (d. c. 160) for example. Marcion saw in Scripture two gods—a god of the Jewish people who created matter and whose legacy was marked by sin and death, war and infidelity, and another god in the Christian writings who was light and healing, truth and liberation, a god who preached peace and salvation. Marcion, therefore, attempted to separate the Old from the New Testaments, denying that the God of Israel could be the God of Christianity. Whereas the God of Genesis immersed us in matter and inevitable destruction upon sending us out from Eden, the God of the Gospels came to free us from this world and to liberate our souls from matter.

Combatting such heresy was Irenaeus's goal in writing his major work, appropriately titled *Against the Heresies*. Defining Christianity as the Son's offering to the Father, he characterized the Catholic faith as a repudiation of all gnostic tendencies which divide God into opposing parts, into a god who creates and another god who saves, a god who wrestles matter into some intelligible form and another god who liberates us from the body and all its travails. Christianity, he argues, teaches the exact opposite. The same Lord who created us is the same Lord who redeems us; the same God who gave each of us our own personalities, quirks, and desires is the same God who longs to consecrate and redeem every aspect of our lives. In Christ, that which the ancient pagan mind found irreconcilable is reconciled and

THE COUNCIL OF NICAEA

made completely one: here heaven and earth meet, divinity and humanity become one, death leads to life, to be great means to serve, to be first is to be last.

The first sustained patristic reflection on the person of Mary came from St. Irenaeus. This is fitting since Irenaeus's entire legacy has to do with making Christians more comfortable with matter, with body, with individuality and with the historical roots of Christ's Church. Irenaeus, therefore, stressed Mary as the New Eve: just as Christ is the New Adam who reenters the human condition to save us from within, Mary, too, gathers all that Eve had destroyed and offers it back to the Father in our name. Think of all the ways Mary fixes what Eve had broken: as Eve listened to a fallen angel, Mary listens to a good angel, as Eve's act brought disobedience and sin, Mary's act brought divine union and salvation, as Eve plucked from the wood of a tree our death, Mary's fruit was restored to that wood, the wood of the cross, so as to bring us everlasting life. As we were all gathered in and descendent from the first Eve on the natural level, on the supernatural level, all Christians are in Mary as their Mother, the one who brings them to Christ. Irenaeus would thus write:

> But Eve was disobedient; for she did not obey when as yet she was a virgin. And even as she, having indeed a husband, Adam, but being nevertheless as yet a virgin, having become disobedient, was made the cause of death, both to herself and to the entire human race; so also did Mary, having a man betrothed [to her], and being nevertheless a virgin, by yielding obedience,

become the cause of salvation, both to herself and the whole human race . . . thus indicating the recapitulation from Mary to Eve, because what is joined together could not otherwise be put asunder than by inversion of the process by which these bonds of union had arisen; so that the former ties be cancelled by the latter, that the latter may set the former again at liberty. And it has, in fact, happened that the first compact looses from the second tie, but that the second tie takes the position of the first which has been cancelled.[53]

Against the gnostic dualism, such a theology of recapitulation gave Irenaeus what he needed to show how God saves as he created, respecting the natures of things and restoring them in a way that fulfills but never destroys them. What the first heads of humanity, Adam and Eve, neglected, the new Adam, Christ, and the new Eve, Mary, now restore and make available again for all: "For it was necessary for Adam to be recapitulated in Christ, that 'mortality might be swallowed up in immortality,' and Eve in Mary, that a virgin, become an advocate for a virgin, might undo and destroy the virginal disobedience by virginal obedience."[54]

God never gives up on his creation. Unlike our generation that just throws something away when it breaks and

---

[53] Irenaeus, *Against Heresies* 3.22; trans. A. Cleveland Coxe, *Ante-Nicene Fathers*, vol. 1, *op. cit.*, p. 455, slightly adjusted. Such theology is the foundation of today's devotion made popular by Pope Francis: Mary, Undoer of Knots.

[54] Irenaeus, *On the Apostolic Preaching*, trans. John Behr (Crestwood, NY: St. Vladimir's Seminary Press, 1997), p. 61.

buys a brand new one, God never tossed us aside but again uses pristine humanity to bring us into union with him. He descends into humanity so as to save us from within; he experiences human life and emotions to show us not only that he loves us but that he is one of us. And at the heart of this love is a woman, Mary, assenting to the Father's invitation to allow his Son to become human, to take on human flesh, to enter the womb from which we all come. This is the humility and the beauty of our God: to save us as he created us, through love, through freedom, through humanity.

In such a theology of recapitulation, we see how the Father never tires of finding ways to bring us into unity with his own life. What divinity over creation failed to achieve, divinity in creation now reconciled: no longer is God "out there," but in this new way of being human modeled perfectly in the New Adam and New Eve, all men and women can see how faith in Christ through his Mother is stronger than the sin and death brought about by our freely chosen disobedience. Mary thus "unties" what Eve had knotted; love again is stronger than death. And it is this sense of liberation which allows Irenaeus to coin what might be his most famous line, usually translated as, *the glory of God is the human person fully alive*, or more literally: "For the glory of God is a living man; and the life of man consists in beholding God. For if the manifestation of God which is made by means of the creation, affords life to all living in the earth, much more does that revelation of the Father which comes through the Word, give life to those who see God."[55]

---

[55] *Against Heresies* 4.20; trans. A. Cleveland Coxe, *Ante-Nicene Fathers*, vol. 1, *op. cit.*, p. 490.

God's glory is his own life in each of us; that which the first Adam and Eve lost has been in fact strengthened even more in the New Adam and Eve. That is why in Irenaeus's method of treating salvation history in terms of all things being renewed by God's envoys, Mother Mary is treated as the New Eve who, through her fiat or "yes," undoes the damage in which the first Eve involved the entire human race. Irenaeus rightly completes Paul's theology of Christ as the New Adam (cf. Rom 5:12–21; 1 Cor 15:22) by seeing in Mary the New Eve, the new Mother of all Christians. Whereas our first (biological) mother fell at the temptation of a (fallen) angel, our Mother in the order of grace fell in love with our Father through the invitation of an angel as well. This sense of Mary's love overturning Eve's aversion would flower into a medieval trope, supplying the imagery for much poetry and song. Think, for instance, of that original woman *Eva*, whose disobedience is reversed by that first Christian word, *Ave . . . Maria, gratia plena*.

Turning to Irenaeus's theology of how Christ unfurls his own life into the lives of his followers, we encounter a robust and rich theology of the Mystical Body. In his theology of recapitulation, Irenaeus stresses the reality that in becoming human, the divine Son of God renders humans divine. He who is Son by nature longs to make other sons and daughters through grace:

> To whom the Word says, mentioning his own gift of grace: I said, *You are all the sons and daughters of the Highest, and gods* (Ps 82:6); but you shall die like men. He speaks undoubtedly these words to those who

have not received the gift of adoption, but who despise the incarnation of the pure generation of the Word of God, defraud human nature of promotion into God, and prove themselves ungrateful to the Word of God, who became flesh for them. For it was for this end that the Word of God was made man, and he who was the Son of God became the Son of man, that man, having been taken into the Word, and receiving the adoption, might become the son or daughter of God. For by no other means could we have attained to incorruptibility and immortality, unless we had been united to incorruptibility and immortality. But how could we be joined to incorruptibility and immortality, unless, first, incorruptibility and immortality had become that which we also are, so that the corruptible might be swallowed up by incorruptibility, and the mortal by immortality, that we might receive the adoption of sons and daughters of God?[56]

As time passed and theologians begin to enjoy more leisure for reflection and collegiality, we will begin to see this theme of divinization unfold more clearly. It is clear that it is a constant already, however, as Irenaeus stresses that out of divine descent, the Son of God "became what we are" so that "he might bring us to be even what he himself is."[57]

In assuming creation to himself, the Creator not only salvages the broken and redeems the sinner, he even elevates

---

[56]   Ibid., 3.19; trans., A. Cleveland Coxe, *Ante-Nicene Fathers*, vol. 1, *op. cit.*, p. 448; slightly adjusted.
[57]   Ibid., 5; *Preface*, p. 526; slightly adjusted.

and transforms the created condition into an intimate other self. This is the ultimate unity and the final goal of Christ's Church: to baptize created souls into the filiality of the Son and thereby through favor, recreate children of men into children of the same heavenly Father and even mother in the order of grace. This is the deified life that Christ's unfurling himself into his followers aims to achieve, and it is a theme that grows more and more explicit and constant as the next centuries themselves unfold.

As we round out our examination of the major figures of the early Church when being Catholic was still illegal and thus punishable, we move from Europe to North Africa. These final three theologians helped the Church in many invaluable ways. While they are not considered Apologists in the strict sense, not having composed treatises to local authorities in order to explain the Catholic faith, they did in fact live during times of persecution and many of their writings are therefore very apologetic in tone. Let us now take up these last three theologians of the third century and see how Christian union is expressed in various ways.

Tertullian of Carthage (d. c. 220)

The first theologian to write exclusively in Latin was Tertullian of Carthage. According to Jerome, who composed a biographical recording of the Church's 135 most influential people—*On Illustrious Men*, dated around 393—Tertullian was:

> the presbyter, now regarded as chief of the Latin writers after Victor and Apollonius, was from the city of

Carthage in the province of Africa, and was the son of a proconsul or Centurion, a man of keen and vigorous character, he flourished chiefly in the reign of the emperor Severus and Antoninus Caracalla and wrote many volumes which we pass by because they are well known to most. . . . He was presbyter of the church until middle life, afterwards driven by the envy and abuse of the clergy of the Roman church, he lapsed to the doctrine of Montanus, and mentions the new prophecy in many of his books.[58]

The heresy Jerome describes here is Montanism. It was a wildly Pentecostal group growing in Asia Minor which stressed prophetic utterances, bouts of ecstatic movement supposedly from the Holy Spirit, the ministry of women priestesses, and other novelties. While we are not sure how or why Tertullian was drawn into this new movement, the fact that he, as such a prolific theologian, had joined caused later churchmen to refer to this group as the "Tertullianists."

Before his lapse into heresy, however, Tertullian the theologian did much to develop the Latin Church's understanding of the Godhead (e.g., the first to use the Latin term *Trinitas*) and to provide the theology supporting numerous perfectly orthodox Church practices such as consecrated celibacy, penance, liturgical garb, fasting, and others. He was also the first to provide a commentary on the Our Father. Since the unity of the Mystical Body is the theme which runs throughout Tertullian's multifaceted

---

[58]   Jerome, *Lives of Illustrious Men* §53; trans. Ernest Cushing Richardson, *Nicene and Post-Nicene Fathers*, vol. 3, *op cit.*, p. 373.

treatises, his apostasy becomes even harder to explain and certainly explains why he is neither a canonized saint nor a Church Father. Yet in his more Catholic phase, we receive wonderful insights on how the unity of the Christian body is key to our own holiness, as we are inextricably interconnected to one another in all belonging in Christ: "The body cannot feel gladness at the trouble of any one member" (1 Cor 12:26). It must necessarily join with one consent in the grief, and in laboring for the remedy. In a company of two is the Church; but the Church is Christ. When, then, you cast yourself at the brethren's knees, you are handling Christ, you are entreating Christ. In like manner, when they shed tears over you, it is Christ who suffers, Christ who prays the Father for mercy. What a son asks is ever easily obtained."[59] Written during his orthodox Catholic phase, Tertullian understood that the Church and Christ are one, and the unity of the Mystical Body is a direct extension of Christ's own divine and human life.

As an interesting aside, we may note that Tertullian may have been the author of the martyrial act of Perpetua and Felicity. North African was susceptible to regional outbursts of persecution against the rapidly growing Christian body. But just after his death, the first-ever imperial wide outbreak occurs under Emperor Decius in 250. In these years, the Lord saw fit to send his Church two of the last great theologians before Christianity's legalization. Different in occupation and temperament, one was a more laconic bishop, the other a wildly fierce theologian. Both

---

[59]　Tertullian, *On Repentance* §10; trans. S. Thelwall, *Ante-Nicene Fathers*, vol. 3, *op. cit.*, p. 664.

men were quintessentially African in their tone and in their courageous explanation of the Faith in the face of fierce opposition. These two titans were Origen of Alexandria and Cyprian of Carthage.

Origen (d. c. 254)

As the pagan attacks against the Church became more systematic and sophisticated, so too did the defenses of the Christian thinkers. Onto this volatile stage strode one of the Church's greatest minds, Origen, nicknamed Adamantus because of his tough—adamant—ascetical and intellectual reputation. He was born around 185 in Alexandria and died around 254 in Tyre after suffering torture during the great persecution of the emperor Decius. To summarize Origen's influence on the Christian intellectual tradition is nearly impossible; suffice to say that he was the first to attempt a systematic presentation of the Faith. His thought was very abstract, and at times, he misconstrued some essential teachings—such as the Trinity or Incarnation—which were defined only more accurately at later Church councils. Yet, it really was Origen's writings which came to teach most of the saints in the early Church. His biblical commentaries set the Church on the course she follows in many ways to this day, a course that takes historical and philological concerns seriously, but which also sees deeper allegory running throughout even the most mundane passages, inviting all readers of Scripture to greater holiness.

One of the last serious anti-Catholic writers of that era was a man named Celsus, who around 180 composed his

On True Doctrine (perhaps aimed at Justin's *Apologies*). Celsus accused Christians of mangling Greek philosophy and of being unable to answer how one man could be the savior of all or why Jesus came so late in time and in such obscure circumstances—lowly, a carpenter's son, a Jew rather than a powerful Roman, wise Athenian, or even a miracle-working Egyptian. The "folly of the Cross," the greatest paradox the world has ever known, was lost upon the intellectuals of the ancient world. But in Origen's response to this pagan polemic, he stresses how the salvation of the world was necessarily achieved by the unification of the heavens and the earth, of the lowly and the Almighty. In so doing, God elevates into heavenly realities by first lowering himself into human tragedies: "Realize that those who in many places teach the doctrine of Jesus rightly and live an upright life are themselves also called Christs by the divine scriptures. . . . That is why, since Christ is the head of the Church, so that Christ and the Church are one body, the oil on the head descended upon the beard of Aaron, the signs of the full-grown man, and why this oil descended till it reached the skirts of his garment."[60]

Christian salvation is much more than simply following the rules or professing some creed; it is to become another Christ, to share in the anointing of the Great High Priest's offering of self to the Father. We again see here how the early theologians of Christ's Church viewed the events of salvation history as extensions of Jesus's own life: the oil of the priesthood is one, running down through the

[60]   Origen, *Contra Celsum*, Bk. 6.79, trans. Henry Chadwick (Cambridge University Press, 1980), p. 392.

foreshadowings of the Old Testament and directly anointing the priests and the people of Christ's Church today. Origen's other great work, *On First Principles*, attempted to provide a coherent account of the nature of God, creation and the fall of humankind, salvation in Christ, and the end times. In these four books, he admits that he is trying to be faithful to the two great pillars of truth, Sacred Scripture and sacred tradition, the only sources for expounding true Christian doctrine. But posterity has not always been sympathetic toward Origen. In his highly speculative approach to the will of God for the salvation of all (Origen seems to argue that even Satan and the fallen angels will eventually be redeemed through the ever-victorious love of Christ), he at times tended to subordinate the Son to the Father which would give later theologians a problem to solve in clarifying the Trinity or an erroneous "proof-text" on which they could base their own heresies.

Origen was a popular, sought-after catechist. After he fell out with his bishop, Demetrius, he was wooed to Caesarea Philippi in 231 where he was eventually ordained by Theoctistus and Alexander of Jerusalem. This caused the Church in Alexandria to disparage Origen publicly, even flaming the infamous rumor of his own castration (his detractors gossiping that Origen took Matthew 19:12 too literally), he was incapable of ever having been ordained over in the competing diocese of Caesarea Philippi. But there he utilized the basic insights of Plato (a later version of them called "Middle Platonism") to start a Christian school of catechetics which was so successful in converting the best and the brightest that he drew the attention of the entire Mediterranean intelligentsia. So, when a disastrous plague broke out in 249, the emperor Decius conveniently blamed the Christians and had Origen imprisoned until he renounced Christ. After two years of torture, he was finally released after Decius was killed in 251. Sometime thereafter, Origen died due to the wounds endured in prison and is thus considered not a martyr but a confessor and someone whose legacy is still being understood and, in some matters, clarified.

Cyprian of Carthage (d. 258)

The plague which occasioned Decius's superstitious lashing out at the Christian Church was actually known as Cyprian's Plague because this well-known bishop of Carthage described its nature and effects so vividly. Cyprian had caught the public imagination. In his letters and theological treatises, we meet one of the last Christian apologists in the times of pagan persecution. Born probably in Carthage around 200, Cyprian went through the normal course of studies, became a very successful courtroom lawyer, and admitted to having lived a lavish and reckless lifestyle in his youth. At some point in his story, Cyprian met a priest who brought him to Christ—Caecilius, the name which Cyprian thereafter adopted for himself—and he left the courts to seek baptism in 245. Pressed into ecclesiastical service, Cyprian became bishop of Carthage, but not without a little resistance and pushback from senior clergy who were suspicious of this all too recent convert.

As mentioned earlier, Cyprian is best known for his work against the Novatianists, a rigorist sect who opposed the return of those Christians who colluded with the Romans during the Decian persecutions. In his defense of the Church's unity and dominical order to be merciful, Cyprian had to fight two battles: one within the Church against those who wanted a pure Church void of all sinners and one without against the veteran pagans who still ran much of Carthage. He wrote to buoy his faithful and give them the courage they needed to stay close to Christ, reminding them, "You cannot have God for your Father if you have not the Church for your Mother."[61] As in any family, these two must complement one another: a God without a Church is an abstraction whom we can shape and fashion in whatever way that is most convenient for our own moral and spiritual lives; a Church without a God is nothing but a human society based on mutual well-wishing. But to enter the true Church is also to become another Christ: "Therefore we accompany Him, we follow Him, we have Him as the Guide of our way, the Source of light, the Author of salvation, promising as well the Father as heaven to those who seek and believe. What Christ is, we Christians shall be, if we imitate Christ."[62]

We become another Christ because he first became one of us. This is a mingling of humanity and divinity which

---

[61] Cyprian, *The Unity of the Catholic Church* §6; trans. Bévenot, *op. cit.*, pp. 48–49; see also CCC §181.

[62] Cyprian of Carthage, "On the Vanity of Idols," *Treatise* 6.15; trans. A. Cleveland Coxe, *Ante-Nicene Fathers*, vol. 5, p. 469.

is represented for our sake at every Holy Mass when the water and wine mingle in the chalice of sacrifice:

> For Christ bore the burden of us all, having borne the burden of our sins. And so we can see that by water is meant God's people, whereas Scripture reveals that by wine is signified the blood of Christ. When, therefore, water is mixed with wine in the cup, the people are made one with Christ and the multitude of believers are bonded and united with Him in whom they have come to believe. . . . Thus there is nothing that can separate the union between Christ and the Church, that is, the people who are established within the Church and who steadfastly and faithfully persevere in their beliefs: Christ and His Church must remain ever attached and joined to each other by indissoluble love.[63]

The hypostatic union of the incarnate Son's humanity and divinity continues in the unity of the Eucharistic sacrifice, which then becomes the promise and pattern of the Christian's communion with Christ. Cyprian's ecclesiology is wholly Eucharistic, as Christ communicates his own sacred body and blood into, and as, the very bodies of his believers.

Cyprian is also a quintessential third-century bishop: the Church is the only way not to be consumed by the storms and the savagery of this fallen world; she is, therefore, to be

---

[63] Cyprian, *Epistle* 63.13.1-2; trans. G. W. Clarke, *The Letters of St. Cyprian of Carthage*, vol. III (New York: Newman Press, 1986), p. 105. See also *ep.* 76 where Cyprian translates the persecution of martyrs into becoming a sacrificial oblation.

tended to and obeyed as one would a loving Mother, and such ecclesial devotion should know absolutely no division: "God is one and Christ is one: there is one Church and one chair founded, by the Lord's authority, upon Peter. It is not possible that another altar can be set up, or that a new priesthood can be appointed, over and above this one altar and this one priesthood. Whoever gathers elsewhere, scatters."[64]

The extant writings of Cyprian bear this ecclesial transformation out. The Church is the indispensable access point to divine grace. Or as he so famously wrote, "Outside the Church, there is no salvation" (*extra ecclesiam, nulla salus*).[65] A line which has caused much theological reflection, discussion, debate, and disputation is Cyprian's simply reminding us that the Church is an established mystical Body which alone can offer the sure salvation of her founder, Jesus Christ. All the ramifications and what that means for a righteous Jew or a God-fearing Buddhist would be questions that ensuing centuries would have to wrestle with, but the writings of Bishop Cyprian—especially his *On the Unity of the Catholic Church*, *On the Lapsed*, and his *Commentary on the Our Father*—still serve as powerful testimonies to Jesus's desire to bring the entire human race into one kingdom, one way of life.

The second and third centuries mark the age of the Apologists. These learned men abandoned sure success in

---

[64]   Cyprian, *Epistle* 43.5.2; trans. G. W. Clarke, *The Letters of St. Cyprian*, *op.cit.*, vol. II (1984), p. 64.
[65]   For the Church's theology of this oftentimes misunderstood phrase, see CCC §846–48.

the world to turn their intellects and rhetorical prowess to the support of Jesus Christ and his Church. They employed the rhetorical and philosophical terms and techniques in which they were trained to demonstrate the reasonableness of the Christian faith. They spent their lives in this way in order to show that the Christian people should be considered, not enemies of the State, but the empire's most loyal and God-fearing citizens. These apologetic writings also attempted to show a world blinded by the harshness of sin the immoralities and inconsistencies of the pagan religions. Finally, these Apologists were never content simply defending the Faith, they also wanted to advance it as well, and they accordingly set out to convert the leading intellects of their time in the hope that the entire known world would come to see how the best of their various cultures had been a share in the Logos all along and could therefore now freely surrender to the God-made-man Jesus Christ.

Constantine and Conversion

The second and third centuries saw the incomparable growth of the Church. From the East came learned converts who sought to bring the Hellenic and Roman mind to Christ. To do this, they had to understand not only the non-Christian worldview but also how best to use the Gospel to show that Christian wisdom did not desire to eradicate the best philosophy of the day but instead to consecrate it and bring it into line with truth eternal. Numbers are not easy to come by, but it is clear that since the year 100, Christians had been adding enough people to their

Body that Church manuals on how to conduct liturgy for a large number of people were required: baptisms increased, Christian neighborhoods arose, and Roman prefects and local governors began to take serious notice. One does not torture something which is not a threat, and Rome saw in the ever-growing Church a serious danger to the *mos maiorum*, its ancient traditions and ways of life that that gave Romans their identity.

However, something happened at the beginning of the fourth century that would transform this story forever. On July 25, 306, the Roman general Constantius was cut down in battle in York, England. His son Constantine proved worthy and was acclaimed the new emperor by the army there. With Roman potentates constantly vying for imperial rule, civil war naturally ensued. Constantine marched into Italy to assume full power, challenging Maxentius, who had just taken the throne to himself. Resting the night before what all knew would be the decisive battle, Constantine and his men took up camp at the Milvian bridge, just north of Rome. According to Lactantius (d. c. 325), a chronicler who was traveling with Constantine on his way down into Italy, the new Roman leader had a divine visitor that evening, a sort of vision which convinced the emperor that his only victory would come through Christ:

> Constantine was directed in a dream to cause *the heavenly sign* to be delineated on the shields of his soldiers, and so to proceed to battle. He did as he had been commanded, and he marked on their shields the letter X, with a perpendicular line drawn through it

and turned round thus at the top, being the cipher of Christ. Having this sign (XP), his troops stood to arms. The enemies advanced, but without their emperor, and they crossed the bridge. The armies met, and fought with the utmost exertions of valour, and firmly maintained their ground. In the meantime a sedition arose at Rome, and Maxentius was reviled as one who had abandoned all concern for the safety of the commonweal; and suddenly, while he exhibited the Circensian games on the anniversary of his reign, the people cried with one voice, Constantine cannot be overcome![66]

According to another historian, this dream was actually a vision perceptible to all who looked heavenwards.

Eusebius of Caesarea notes that Constantine was looking up into the sky, "about noon, when the day was already beginning to decline; he saw with his own eyes the trophy of a cross of light in the heavens, above the sun, and bearing the inscription, *Conquer by this*. At this sight he himself was struck with amazement, and his whole army also, which followed him on this expedition, and witnessed the miracle."[67] This affirming miracle of the phrase *In Hoc Signo Vinces* ("In this sign you shall conquer") some say gave rise to the symbol IHS so prevalent in Christian decoration and architecture (when in reality those are also the first three letters in Greek of Jesus's name, IHSOUS). But an endur-

---

[66]　Lactantius, *On the Deaths of the Persecutors* §44; trans. William Fletcher, *Ante-Nicene Fathers*, vol. 7, *op. cit.*, p. 318.
[67]　Eusebius, *Life of Constantine* §28; trans. Arthur Cushman McGiffert, *Nicene and Post-Nicene Fathers*, vol. 1, *op. cit.*, p. 490.

ing legend has arisen around this moment in Christian history: for whatever happened that night or day, however this vision is replicated in Christian art and iconography, we do know for sure that something happened to Constantine before the battle, his victory in which made him sole ruler of the Western empire, and that upon his defeat of Maxentius, he gave credit to the God of the Christians and almost immediately set out to let the Christians worship without fear.

Most practically, Constantine and his co-emperor in the East, Licinius, declared that Christians should be able to worship freely and that all persecutions against them should cease. Even though Licinius would soon renege on his end of this bargain, in 313 the two emperors signed what we now know as the Edict of Milan which (in part) states:

> When we, Constantine and Licinius, Emperors, met at Milan in conference concerning the welfare and security of the realm, we decided that of the things that are of profit to all mankind, the worship of God ought rightly to be our first and chiefest care, and that it was right that Christians and all other should have the freedom to follow the kind of religion they favored; so that the God who dwells in heaven might be propitious to us and to all under our rule.... Moreover, concerning the Christians, we before gave orders with respect to the places set apart for their worship. It is now our pleasure that all who have bought such

places should restore them to the Christians, without
any demand for payment.[68]

From AD 313 onward, we see that Christians were to be
treated just like all other licit cults: free to worship as they
saw fit and to hold property and not to be harried by any
other group. We also see that Constantine's legitimization
of the Catholic faith was done not out of devotion or piety
but out of that same Roman need to ensure proper worship
for the civic good. Constantine was not yet a man of the
Church, but he was on his way.

At the beginning of the fourth century Christians are
still a small minority within the empire, maybe 15 percent of
the population, so the work of evangelization has only just
begun. The reign of Constantine (306–37) was an extremely
important time for the Church in this regard. Constantine
is not only responsible for legalizing Christianity, he also
became a convert and was received into the very Church he
came to love and defend. For Constantine saw in his role
as emperor the God-given duty to foster Church unity and
defend the Faith from noxious aberrations. This became
most manifest at the Council of Nicaea in 325 when Constantine called for, and ruled over, the Church's first ecumenical council.

---

[68]   Lactantius reproduces the Edict of Milan in full in his *On the
Deaths of the Persecutors* §48; cf., Bettenson, *Documents of the Christian
Church, op. cit.*, pp. 15–16.

He Will Guide You to All Truth

THE GREEK FATHERS AND THE FIRST COUNCIL OF CONSTANTINOPLE (381)

"I have yet many things to say to you, but you cannot bear them now. When the Spirit of truth comes, he will guide you into all the truth; for he will not speak on his own authority, but whatever he hears he will speak, and he will declare to you the things that are to come. He will glorify me, for he will take what is mine and declare it to you. All that the Father has is mine; therefore I said that he will take what is mine and declare it to you" (Jn 16:12–15).

THE ONE TRUE Teacher, Christ reveals the fullness of God slowly and carefully: "Let not your hearts be troubled; believe in God, believe also in me" (Jn 14:1). He knows his Jewish followers already have faith in God, and their strict monotheistic creed proves to be one of the great gifts Judaism will ever give the world of religions. Jesus could not risk upsetting the unparalleled *Shema Yisrael*—"Hear, O Israel: The LORD our God is one LORD" (Dt 6:4; Mk 12:29). Yet he hints at another divine person to come, a Spirit who will eventually show his followers the truest nature of God's very being as a Trinity of Perfect Persons.

But who is Jesus to summarize the entirety of Judaism in this way? Not only does he never definitively define his godliness, but in plain speech he even seems to contradict any such notion. "Why do you call me good? No one is good but God alone" (Lk 18:19), says the supposed Son of God. "You heard me say to you, 'I go away, and I will come to you.' If you loved me, you would have rejoiced, because I go to the Father; for the Father is greater than I" (Jn 14:28), says one whom the Church declares *consubstantial* with the Father. Jesus left it to his Church to figure out the mysteries of the Trinity as much as creatures can, pondering deeply the truths and significance of a God who dwells in three Divine Persons.

It is precisely this unity that provides the thesis of this book: made in the image and likeness of a Triune God (Gn 1:26–27), the human person becomes truly him or herself only in union with the other. Think of the utter interpersonal dependence of the Trinity: the Father is who he is as Father only because he has a Son, the Son is who he is as Son only because he has been begotten eternally by the Father. These relationships *do not simply affect* who Father, Son, and Holy Spirit are in the same way relationships affect us creatures; *these relationships utterly effect* who each divine Person is as "Father," "Son," and "Holy Spirit," and this wholly oth-er-centeredness of each divine Person is the pattern for a full life for those made in the image of the Triune God as well. Any lover knows this: as long as we live only for our own well-being, we become cold and cheap; yet, when we begin to surrender to another, we begin to see the beauty and blessedness of human existence, of what it means to be a person "fully alive." It may take a while to realize that the other who alone can truly fulfill us is the Lord Jesus Christ—maturing our way through various other attempts at finding wholeness—but when we finally come to soften spiritually and surrender before his godly gaze, we begin to understand what it means to be a person fully alive, someone whose identity is bound up with another outside him or herself. That is why relationship is risky; we ourselves are no longer at the definitive center of things.

This chapter accordingly focuses on how the Church came to understand that the one true God is a community of love, three divine Persons sharing perfectly in the essence of godliness in three different ways. While a mainstay of theological reflection since Jesus Christ commissioned his Church to go and baptize in those three names "of the Father and of the Son and of the Holy Spirit" (Mt 28:19), the doctrine of the Trinity received its first official attention at the Council of Nicaea in 325. We begin with the first ecumenical council which clarified Trinitarian thought and thereby solidified the desired unity Constantine wanted for his Church as well as his empire. From there we shall then move through the fourth century, examining the major figures who helped move the Church from Apology to more systematic, if not sophisticated, theological analysis. Now theologians could meet openly, hold synods, develop civic canons, and begin to theologize without worry of imperial retribution. Or so they thought.

As we just rehearsed in chapter 2, Christianity was an illicit religion until 313. With Constantine's legalization of the Faith, the Church was now able to gather publicly and settle matters of disputed doctrine. With the threat of persecution abated (for the most part), the Church was able to raise up theologians who were able to excel in developing a more speculative theology, magisterial doctrine, and more uniform prayer and liturgies. At the Council of Nicaea, for instance, the young deacon Athanasius emerged victorious from so many scuffles.

Also considered will be the theological contributions of the great Cappadocian Fathers—Basil the Great (d. 379), his younger brother Gregory of Nyssa (d. 395), and Gregory of Nazianzus (d. 389)—before moving to the First Council of Constantinople. We will then conclude with a quick study of St. John Chrysostom (d. 407), whose preaching and exhortations to holiness made him one of the great Greek Fathers of the Church.

For centuries, early Christianity remained a Greek phenomenon: Mass was celebrated in Greek, prayers were recited in Greek, the Scriptures remained in Greek. Even in Rome all things Catholic were offered in the intellectual language of the Mediterranean world until Pope Damasus (366–84) commissioned a young priest by the name of Jerome, at the end of the fourth century, to translate the canonical books, the creeds, and the liturgy into an accessible Latin. The greatest of these early Greek thinkers gave the Church the imagery and vocabulary with which to best understand the Trinity and the Incarnation.

Constantine and the Council of Nicaea

When we turn to the significant Church events of the fourth century, we almost always find ourselves in modern-day Turkey, where the first major Church councils were held, where the great theologians of the oriental age thrived, and where the foundational theologies of God were worked out for the rest of the Tradition. These parts of Asia Minor had become so central to the way people—Christian and non-Christian alike—saw themselves and the best of their various cultures that in 330 Constantine moved the imperial palace to the center of Greek intellectual life and renamed Byzantium as his own city, Constantinople.

Located on the European side of the Straits of Bosporus, Constantinople became "the New Rome" and vied against Italy in setting the cultural and ecclesial tone of the next couple of centuries. It would be in the long-casting shadow of this great city that both the Son (at Nicaea in 325) and the Holy Spirit (at I Constantinople in 381) would be declared consubstantial with the Father, where Mary was named the Mother of God (at Ephesus in 431), and where the dual-natured life of Christ, fully God and fully human, was officially worked out (at Chalcedon in 451).

One of Constantine's first initiatives as emperor was to fund the building of Christian churches, giving the Lateran Palace in Rome to the pope, for example, as well as numerous other instances in Jerusalem and in his new eponymous city. But more than just helping to fix Christianity on the physical landscape of the empire, Constantine also began

to enshrine Christian ethics into law: he abolished the crucifixion of criminals for sport, piously arguing that Jesus
Christ should be the last one on earth ever to die in that
way; he forbade the branding of slaves on their faces, seeing
that there is where we most image God; and he amelio-
rated prison conditions across the empire. Also, he not only
curtailed a slave owner's "rights" over his slaves, he declared
Sunday to be sabbath rest for all.

Although he would not seek baptism until just a few
days before his death in May of 337, Constantine was clearly
on the side of the Christian people, and a new chapter in
Church history had begun. Sensing the inevitable growth
of the Catholic Church, Constantine knew it was in his
best interest that this influential group stay united in essential matters of doctrine. Leading up to the historic Council
of Nicaea in 325, the major doctrinal concern from which
theological factions arose was the question of how the persons of the Godhead were related. There was no Christian
who did not know and accept Jesus's mandate to baptize
"in the name of the Father and of the Son and of the Holy
Spirit" (Mt 28:19), but what was meant by each of these
names and how they all might be related gave rise to many
discussions and disagreements before Nicaea.

A pressing concern for centuries was the question of
how it could be maintained that Son of God could be God
without falling into polytheism. Nicaea served to put an
end to a safely popular theology known as Monarchianism, in which the "arche," or leading principle, was surely
and absolutely one (*monos* in Greek). Modalistic Monarchianism argued that this One God could appear in history

under three different "modes," as Father in the Old Testament, as Son in the New, and as the Holy Spirit in the age of the Church. Such a depiction safeguarded God's unity but could not explain how this one God could exist as three distinct and different Persons. So how could sophisticated theologians be more faithful to a proper reading of the Bible and to the Tradition being built up in the Church's worship and dogma? Another answer arose, Dynamic Monarchianism. In this heresy of Adoptionism, the Father dynamically incorporates this man Jesus Christ into the Trinity, adopting him as his son usually at the moment of his baptism in the Jordan River. Both these forms of Unitarianism were ultimately discarded as not only too facile but unfaithful to the real divine drama depicted in Scripture.

After these tendencies were more or less corrected over the decades of the late second and third centuries, another popular Trinitarian solution arose at the start of the fourth century, and this came to the fore with the pastor of one of the most influential parishes in one of the most influential dioceses. Arius (256–336), pastor of the Baucalis—the bustling Church in Alexandria built over the revered place of the Apostle Mark's martyrdom—could not reconcile his bishop Alexander's preaching on the other side of town that the Son of God was as fully divine as God the Father. Would this not result in polytheism? Would this not break up the essential unity of the Godhead and bifurcate the great gift of Monotheism God had revealed to his first chosen people? Instead, Arius proposed, the Son of God is precisely that: a Son who is surely our savior and who is in fact divine, he simply is not *as divine* as the Father from whom he comes. By definition, Arius argued, God cannot have any sort of beginning, and since the Son is clearly "begotten," he must be a lesser divine person than the Monarch who begets him. Therefore, Arius taught that we must honor and love the Son Jesus Christ, but we must refrain from thinking of him as the exact same nature as the Father. He is instead, he argued, of like nature as the Father.

As tensions arose, Arius began to preach more and began to network with many influential bishops from the East who also found this easy solution to any Trinitarian depth appealing. The easier formula which was proposed by Arius was to conceive of the Son as someone who simply "was not" before he was brought into existence by the Father, rendering him a lesser kind of deity: "We are persecuted because we say, 'The Son has a beginning, but God is without beginning'."[69] For this reason, Arius and his cohorts vehemently denied that the Son and the Father could be of the same substance, of the same nature, that both could be God fully and equally. To argue this way, these later-called "Arians" could draw from Origen who also at times subordinated the Son to the Father, understanding the Father to be God in and of himself, deeming the Son godly only in so far as he partook of the life of the Father.

As it is so crucial to the entire Christian faith, this theology had to be clarified. Since it was much easier to grasp Arius's formulation than the Trinitarian formula of Father,

---

[69] "The Letter of Arius to Eusebius of Nicomedia," trans. Edward Hardy, *Christology of the Later Fathers* (London: Westminster John Knox Press, 1954), pp. 330–31; preserved originally in Theodoret, *Historia Ecclesiastica* [*HE*] 1.4.

Son, and Holy Spirit all being co-equally and consubstantially God without reservation, Arius's aberration became popular with many Christians content with easy answers. This was something that had to be addressed before the rift across the major Catholic dioceses grew wider, and Constantine therefore called a council. This would stand as the first universal gathering of its sort, convening bishops from all over the known world, not just some from a particular region. Coming together at a small town in the middle of modern-day Turkey, the Council of Nicaea is therefore termed the "first ecumenical council," with historians usually providing 318 as the number in attendance (but 318 is symbolically used as the number of Abraham's servants referenced in Genesis 14:14), while in fact, there were probably about 250 bishops gathered. Arius was called to defend his view against his accuser Bishop Alexander of Alexandria, but it would be the bishop's deacon and theologian who would emerge from this clash as an international figure, St. Athanasius of Alexandria.

Athanasius was a most legendary figure. He was a force, known favorably by some "The Church's Pillar" and *Athanasius Contra Mundum* ("Athanasius Against the World" for his five exiles over seventeen years on account of his Christological orthodoxy), and as "the Black Dwarf" by his enemies who wanted to ridicule his diminutive (and dark) stature. Regardless of an epithet, the fourth-century debates over the proper understanding of the Son of God owes everything to this dynamic thinker. Athanasius's life story was marked by condemnations as well as the culminating triumph of canonization—a saint who was pilloried most

of his life for his insistence that Jesus Christ is consubstantial and thus coequal to God the Father, and that the Catholic Church should suffer no division. For Athanasius, these
were truths on which human salvation hung: if Jesus is not
fully God, then he remains just another prophet, height-
ened in human estimation but still himself in need of a true
deity to save him. In stressing the consubstantiality of the
Father and the Son, Athanasius insisted that Jesus Christ
does not simply point us to the Father, but in his incarnation, we too have become children through adoption of the
same heavenly Father.

Athanasius thus maintained that if Christ was in fact
the Savior of the human race, he had to be of the same
divine substance as the Father. But, Arius retorted, if God
the Father is God and his Son is also as fully God, does
that not make two gods? And this is precisely where Athanasius went to work, insisting that the difference between
the Father and the Son was not one of *what* they are—their
substance—but in *who* they are to one another, one being
God the Father and the other being God the Son. To solidify this relationship, Athanasius insisted upon on the Greek
term for being of an equal nature with another—*homo*,
meaning same in Greek, and *ousia*, denoting the "nature" or
"substance" of a thing. Accordingly, *homoousios* became the
catchword of the fourth century, the term insisted upon in
the creed which emerged from Nicaea ("*consubstantial* with
the Father") and the term that became the litmus test for a
theologian's faithfulness.

On the other side of this debate remained the priest
Arius and a growing gathering of bishops who agreed his

view of the Son of God as *homoi*—or like—God the Father in substance. Only this slight subordinationism would ensure the unity and transcendence of the one true God. For Arius had always been insistent that the Son of God, who comes from and therefore after the Father, is very much like the Father in substance, but in no way could be identical to God the Father. Arius's preferred term for this relationship was therefore *homoiousios* from *homoi*, meaning "like" or "similar to," and the standard term for substance, *ousia*.

Arius's theology spread throughout the empire, and Constantine, being an opportunist if nothing else, knew some order and unity had to be brought to the Church, for as the Church went, so would his empire; as long as his most faithful and fruitful demographic, the Christian people, was divided, so would his ability to rule be as well. He therefore insisted that the bishops of the known world should gather after Easter of 325. The council convened under the priestly patronage of Hosius of Cordoba (257–359), Constantine's aged confidant and theological advisor, and examined the differences between Arian and the Alexandrian Christologies. After weeks of debate, the council emerged with the first ever binding formula, the Creed or Symbol of Nicaea. In combatting the Arian subordinationism, the Nicene Creed famously insisted that:

> We believe in one God Father Almighty Maker of all things, visible and invisible;
>
> And in one Lord Jesus Christ the Son of God, begotten as only-begotten of the Father,

> God of God, Light of Light, true God of true God, begotten not made, consubstantial (*homoousios*) with the Father, through whom all things came into existence, both things in heaven and on earth . . .
>
> And in the Holy Spirit.

And then, to make sure that considering the Son any less or any later than the Father was clearly condemned, the Council Fathers added:

> But those who say, (1) "there was a time when he did not exist," and (2) "before being begotten he did not exist," and that (3) "he came into being from non-existence," or who allege that (4) "the Son of God is another *hypostasis* or *ousia*, or is alterable or changeable," these the Catholic and Apostolic Church condemns.

Notice how the pro-Nicene bishops express the Son's relationship with the Father: he is begotten, not made, meaning he is of the same divine substance as the Father. Just as humans beget human children, the divine Father has begotten a divine Son. When? Before all ages! This is a timeless generation, an eternal begetting, as there was never a time the Father was not with the Son, a reality which Arius and his followers just could not comprehend. This Son is, of course, the same God and the same Light, true God from true God, therefore one in the same being or, in Latin, consubstantial with the Father, having the same substance, same nature.

What Nicaea showed was that while there was no doubt that Christ was the long-awaited Messiah, exactly how this wonder-worker and God-made-man was to be understood as incarnately divine stood in need of rigorous and prayerful reflection. Was Jesus as fully divine as the Father or was he to be understood as a lesser type of deity? Nicaea came out quite clearly. The Son of God is an eternally begotten divine person, the Second Person of the Trinity and therefore no less divine than the Father. One thus in being with the Father, in the womb of Mary Jesus Christ became consubstantial with his mother as well. Consequently, Jesus is fully divine and fully human. Precisely how this two-natured divine Person would be explained would be left to later councils, but Nicaea now made it clear that the Son and the Father were co-equal in divinity and therefore co-equally worthy of our praise. In taking on a human nature, the divine Son began to live his perfection in a wholly human way, but this neither lessened his divinity nor did it bifurcate the Godhead.

But whereas one would hope Nicaea answered Arius's concerns, he in fact used his powerful political influence only to foment this fissure, opening up a century-long debate on exactly what the more intricate terms like *homo* and *ousia* meant exactly. As in most ecclesial events, pride and politics were always present, with no faction backing down. Every decade of the fourth century thus saw a few local synods and regional councils in both the eastern and the western provinces. In fact, in the year 359 after one of these regional gatherings, St. Jerome wrote that, "The whole world groaned, and was astonished to find itself Arian."[70] So thank God for heroic bishops like Athanasius. He doggedly insisted on the equality of the Father and the Son, but his episcopacy was about much more than the struggle against Arianism: he also wrote the first Christian biography on the great desert father, St. Antony the Monk; he was the first to publish an official list of the canonical books to be included (and excluded) from the Church's Scriptures, and he fostered in his writings a beautiful image of the unfurled Christ, a loving, humble Son who, as he expressed it, "became human so humans can become God."[71]

In our study, we have seen this theology of deification as early as Ignatius of Antioch, and as with all Christian truth, it remains with us today. It is the ultimate unfolding of Christ into the Christian, a transformative bond so tight that the otherwise sinful and stumbling mortal begins to become an immortal child of the same divine Father and human mother. Even today the Catholic Church relies on Athanasius in its central teaching on why the Word became flesh:

> The Word became flesh to make us "partakers of the divine nature" (2 Pet 1:4): "For this is why the Word became man, and the Son of God became the Son of man: so that man, by entering into communion with the Word and thus receiving divine sonship, might become a son of God" (St. Irenaeus). "For the Son of

70 Jerome, *Dialogue Against the Luciferians*, §19; trans. W. H. Fremantle, *Nicene and Post-Nicene Fathers*, vol. 6, p. 329.
71 Athanasius, *On the Incarnation* §54.3.

God became man so that we might become God" (St. Athanasius). "The only-begotten Son of God, wanting to make us sharers in his divinity, assumed our nature, so that he, made man, might make men gods" (St. Thomas Aquinas).[72]

Note the constant and unbroken trajectory of the ways Christ pours his life into those who surrender to him. As major theologians and saints have taught (and lived) throughout the centuries, Jesus Christ founded a Church so he would have a visible locus, a freely-chosen Body, into whom he could extend his life. We see biblical authors, Church Fathers, medieval Doctors, and modern theologians teaching what Athanasius put most succinctly: God became a man in Jesus Christ so that in Jesus Christ men and women may become "gods." This may be just one metaphor of Christ's unfurling his life into ours, but it certainly is the culmination of Christian discipleship—deification, divinization, *theosis* (the Greek term), to become another Christ!

The incorruptible, immortal, and wholly divine Son of God became human in order to enter into all that is human and thus to consecrate those who freely chose to surrender to him. In this exchange, Christ's humanity for the Christian's divinity, men and women are now able to live no longer as merely earthly, biological creatures. We are invited to live a godly life doing things that no pure creature can, like love one's enemies and suffer injustices charitably, live forever in perfect joy, and so on. In his description of this

---

[72]   CCC §460.

transformation, Athanasius also came to emphasize how the Holy Spirit is that Divine Person who unites the fallen humanity of believers with the sacred humanity of Christ. In this "spiritualization" in which men and women are empowered to live as children of the Father, they come to participate in God's very life in a creaturely and gifted manner (we "partake" of the divine nature, we never "possess" it). This is why Athanasius risked his life to teach that the Son and the Holy Spirit must be as divine, consubstantial/*homoousios* with the Father: for it is the Son and the Spirit who are as active as the Father in saving the human race. We pray to them, we impart their indwelling through the Church's sacraments, we call them Lord and Savior.

For example, in his important *Letters to Serapion* which deal with the divine mission of the Holy Spirit, the saintly bishop of Alexandria showed the Church that if it is the Spirit who makes mortals graced gods, the Spirit himself must be God: "And it is through the Spirit that all of us are said to be partakers of God. . . . If the Holy Spirit were a creature, we would not have participation in God through him. But if we were joined to a creature, we would become strangers to the divine nature inasmuch as we did not partake of it in any way. . . . But if we become *sharers of the divine nature* (2 Pet 1:4) by partaking of the Spirit, someone would have to be insane to say that the Spirit has a created nature and not the nature of God."[73] Looking back over the Church's tumultuous fourth century, we can read the works

---

[73]   Athanasius, *Letter to Serapion* 1.24; trans. Mark DelCogliano et al., *Works of the Holy Spirit: Athanasius the Great and Didymus the Blind* (Yonkers, NY: St. Vladimir's Seminary Press, 2011), p. 90.

of Athanasius of Alexandria as the theology which helped (eventually) settle how the Father and the Son were both equally God, as well as the important work which started to answer this same question for the Holy Spirit.

After Nicaea in 325, the next ecumenical council would be the first at Constantinople in 381, convened by the very Catholic-friendly Emperor Theodosius the First (d. 395) in order both to reaffirm the teachings of Nicaea as well as show how the Third Person of the Trinity is also God. In these intervening decades, God raised up a new generation of theologians who incorporated Athanasius's insights and developed their own way of speaking about Christ and salvation in him. These men, two brothers and a close friend known to us today as the Cappadocian Fathers (so-called after that middle part of modern-day Turkey), were uniquely poised to combat the heresies that continued after Arius's death and to lead the Church into a deeper understanding of the Trinity.

The Cappadocian Fathers

Saints Basil (d. 379) and Gregory (d. 394) were brothers born into an aristocratic Catholic family of nine children, boasting five saints who are all revered still today in the East. Basil was born just before the year 330 and Gregory two years later. Their sister St. Macrina the Younger (d. 379) was an influential virgin, their brothers were St. Naucratius, a hermit about whom not much is known, and St. Peter of Sebaste (d. 391), who became a reforming bishop through-out ancient Armenia. Their father, Basil the Elder, wanted to make sure that his children enjoyed the best education possible and sent the eldest, Basil, to Athens where he dedicated himself to his studies for six years. There Basil met another eager scholar who would soon become his best friend, Gregory from Nazianzus (d. 390). As we see with most friendships between saints, the bond between Basil and Gregory was life-giving and formative for both. Saints are never made in isolation, and together these two were immersed in Greek philosophy and rhetoric with the goal of using it for the sake of the Gospel, to elucidate Christian truths, and to explain the Catholic creed more coherently. Basil even ended up writing a famous treatise *To Young Men on Reading Greek Literature*, exemplifying how early Christianity was eager to learn from the great non- and pre-Christian minds wherever they discerned and encountered the Truth.

In 355, when Basil was just twenty-five or twenty-six, he returned home to teach for a year. But he grew restless, longing to experience firsthand what he had heard about the monastic life which was springing up in Syria, Jerusalem, and Egypt. Basil traveled throughout these countries to investigate and learn from many solitary hermits who would explain to him their desire to live in the desert with such zeal. Upon returning, Basil began a small monastic community and drew up his own rule, a rule that is still used today in many religious houses. A monastery wall cannot hide a young man of Basil's caliber very long, however. In 360, he was sought out for priestly ordination; by 364, the bishop of Caesarea made him his auxiliary bishop with hopes of staving off the extreme Arian views of the emperor

Valens. By 370, Basil had become the metropolitan bishop of all of Cappadocia and had composed many important works: *On the Holy Spirit*, his *Hexaemeron* or commentary on the days of creation, and his essential *Against Eunomius*, wherein he combats the last vestiges of the Arian tendency to subordinate the Son to the Father. More than a speculative scholar, Basil also started some of the first Christian hospitals, using his role as bishop to care for the outcasts and the weak of society.

Basil's younger brother, Gregory, did not follow his brother to Athens for school but stayed closer to home, studying only in Cappadocia. Regardless, of the three Cappadocian Fathers, this Gregory, who comes to be known as "Gregory of Nyssa" due to his becoming bishop of Nyssa in 371, proved to be the most mystical and theologically developed of the three. We know that Gregory was married and did not join his brother Basil and Gregory of Nazianzus in their monastic endeavors but instead was ordained in 372 for the small hamlet of Nyssa in Cappadocia. Perhaps overly contemplative for administrative affairs, Gregory was a bit of a disappointment as a bishop and was deposed by those Arians who still maintained significant ecclesio-political power there. Returning to Nyssa two years later, Gregory's theological sophistication and care for souls won many back to the Faith. His very early treatise *On Virginity* held up the beauty of the consecrated life, his commentary on creation *On the Making of Man* worked through the splendor of Genesis, his *Great Catechism* was used successfully for catechumens. His biographies, *Life of Macrina* and *The Life of Moses*, rely on the use of narrative to tell alluring and memorable stories of how God alone can satisfy any life and that fostering a deep sense of Christian contemplation while on earth is the only way to long for the full glories of heaven even now.

Gregory of Nazianzus was born around 325 in the same town where he died in 389. This seemingly minor detail provides a glimpse into Gregory's personality. Whereas Basil was a savvy administrator and Gregory of Nyssa a much-sought-after speculative theologian, Gregory of Nazianzus had more the heart of a poet and an anchorite, satisfied with his prayers and the simplicity of the monastic life. As mentioned, he met Basil in Athens while studying there as a young man. After finishing his education, Gregory returned to his parents' home in Nazianzus in Cappadocia. In 372, Gregory was made a bishop over the see of Sasima. This see was created by Basil as part of his effort to establish more and more Catholic bishops against Arian episcopacies which were still holding on after Nicaea. Gregory Nazianzen instinctually trusted Basil and he went to Sasima out of his devotion to the Church. Gregory soon realized, however, that this city was a detestable place utterly void of any real civilization. Gregory soon grew despondent and resentful, thereby refusing to reside in Sasima, feeling more like a pawn in imperial politics than a people's needed bishop. Against Basil's wishes, Gregory turned his back on his diocese and returned to Nazianzus, where he would produce some of the most beautiful poems and orations in all of Christian literature, theological orations which provide the basis for so much later thinking on the nature of God, as well as important treatises helping future generations to think rightly about the dual natures of Jesus Christ.

Each in his own way, Basil and the two Gregories understood Christianity as our own personal incorporation into the mystical body of Jesus while on earth. Basil emphasized its effects in elevating our human abilities and actions, Nazianzen emphasized the great exchange, and Gregory of Nyssa stressed our mystical union. Basil's most influential treatise leading up to the First Council of Constantinople's declaration of the Holy Spirit's *homoousios* with the Father and the Son was his *On the Holy Spirit*, outlining the correct way to think about and to invoke, to pray to, and adore the Holy Spirit. Here Basil stresses how we embodied persons are in need of the Holy Spirit to become fully ourselves, teaching that the Spirit alone can allow believers to live out the demands of the Gospel: "The Spirit illuminates those who have been cleansed from every stain and makes them spiritual by means of communion with himself. . . . Just so are the Spirit-bearing souls that are illuminated by the Holy Spirit: they are themselves made spiritual, and they send forth grace to others. Thence comes foreknowledge of the future, understanding of mysteries, apprehension of secrets, distribution of graces, heavenly citizenship, the chorus with angels, unending joy, remaining in God, kinship with God, and the highest object of desire, becoming God."[74]

Eternally, the Spirit is the divine person who unites Father and Son; he is the Love binding God the Lover with God the Beloved. In time, then, the Spirit's role is also

---

[74]   Basil the Great, *On the Holy Spirit* §9.23; trans. Stephen M. Hildebrand (Yonkers, NY: St. Vladimir's Press, 2011), p. 54.

to unite persons—to unite the fragmentation of the individual brought about by sin, to unite persons into Christ's Church, and to bring members of that Church into union with God's own transforming and deifying life.

We have seen how Basil stresses the role of the Holy Spirit as the one person of the Trinity who unites us back to God the Son and in so doing makes each of us into a son or daughter of the same Father: "Through the Holy Spirit comes the restoration to paradise, the ascent to the kingdom of heaven, the return to adopted sonship, the freedom to call God our Father and to become a companion of the grace of Christ, to be called a child of the light."[75]

For Gregory Nazianzen, the Holy Spirit's ability to spiritualize us fallen mortals and thereby raise us up into the eternal glory of God is proof of his divinity. If the Spirit can deify and is not in need of deification, he must be divine. If he did not come into being but brings us contingent beings into eternal life, he must be eternal: "If he did not exist from the beginning, he has the same rank as I have, though with a slight priority—we are both separated from God by time. If he has the same rank as I have, how can he make me a god, how can he link me with deity?"[76] This "linking" for Nazianzen is usually explained through the biblical metaphor of the great exchange: the Son's poverty for our richness (2 Cor 8:9). The initiative of this exchange is of

---

[75]   Basil, *On the Holy Spirit* §15.36; trans. Hildebrand, *op, cit.*, p. 68; see also CCC §736.

[76]   Gregory of Nazianzus, *Oration* §31.4; trans. Fredrick Williams and Lionel Wickham, *On God and Christ*, (Crestwood, NY: St. Vladimir's Press, 2002), p. 119.

course God's, but in his generous kenosis, we are filled with his own life:

> Let us become like Christ, since Christ also became like us; let us become gods because of him, since he also because of us became human. He assumed what is worse that he might give us what is better. He became poor that we through his poverty might become rich (2 Cor 8:9). He took the form of a slave (Phil 2:7), that we might regain freedom. He descended that we might be lifted up, he was tempted that we might be victorious, he was dishonored to glorify us, he died to save us, he ascended to draw to himself us who lay below in the Fall of sin. Let us give everything, offer everything, to the one who gave himself as a ransom and an exchange for us (Mt 20:28). But one can give nothing comparable to oneself, understanding the mystery and becoming because of him everything that he became because of us.[77]

This goal of becoming godly by being incorporated into the great exchange of God's humanity for our divinity was even more of a theme in the theology of Basil's brother Gregory of Nyssa. Like his brother Basil, Gregory of Nyssa was constantly immersed in the Trinitarian debates of the fourth century; he provides with the following anecdote that shows how the most abstract theological speculations trickled down to the most common of conversations throughout the city streets: "The entire town—the public squares, the

---

[77] Gregory of Nazianzus, *Oration* §1.5; trans., Nonna Verna Harrison, *Festal Orations* (Crestwood, NY: St Vladimir's Press 2008) 59.

marketplaces, the cross-roads and alleys—are full of this din. Tailors, bankers, restauranteurs are all busy arguing. So, if you ask someone to make change, he will philosophize over the Begotten and the Unbegotten. If you ask a baker how much for a loaf of bread, he will tell you that the Father has to be greater than a Son who is subordinate. If you ask an attendant at the baths if your water is ready, he will tell you that, 'Son was made out of nothing.'"[78]

But theology never remained abstract for Gregory of Nyssa, as mystical as his tendencies are. He always sought to translate theological dogma into a sort of ecclesial devotion. While he did find some popular practices which were just coming into vogue, like pilgrimages to the Holy Land, Gregory Nyssen was intent on leading others into a seriously profound interiority through which any man or woman could come to realize his or her great vocation for holiness.

Among Gregory's lasting contributions, then, was his insistence, along with Athanasius and other great Church Fathers, that God became human so that humans could become like God. Gregory thus emphasized, whenever he could, the need for our understanding that true human perfection consists not in rule-keeping or intelligence only.

---

[78]   Gregory of Nyssa, *Oration on the Divinity of the Son and of the Holy Spirit*, *Patrologia Graeca* 46. 557B; my translation. Throughout the middle of the nineteenth century, a French polymath, Fr. Jacques Paul Migne (d. 1875), collected all the then available Church Fathers and produced a 165 volume work of the Greek Fathers, the *Patrologia Graeca* [PG], as well as a 221 volume work of the Latin Fathers, the *Patrologia Latina* [PL]; despite some newer, more critical series today, many primary texts are still available only in this remarkable series.

It was only by our surrender and consequent participation in the life of Christ offered only through his Church that we mortals become whole. This is a union sought not only between Jesus and the individual believer but among all, because all of God's children were originally created to be a harmonious-diversity-in-loving-unity: "Since by participation we are joined to the one Body of Christ, we all become one body, his own. When we shall have all become perfect, then his whole body will be subject to the life-giving power. The surrender of this body is called the surrender of the Son himself since he is united with his body, which is the Church."[79] This mystical identity is the bedrock of Gregory's soteriology: we are saved because we have become one with Christ.

This notion of "surrender" is a key factor in explaining how Christ unfurls himself into the lives of his followers. As the Father has poured all he is into his Only Begotten, the Son of God takes all of humanity into himself when he assumes the fullness of our nature. He is the New Adam who has come into the Father's vineyard to graft all the stray vines of the human condition onto himself:

> Sine he is all in all, he takes into himself all who are united with him by the participation of his body; he makes them all members of his body, in such wise that the many members are but one body. Having thus united us with himself and himself with us, and

---

[79]   Gregory of Nyssa, *In Illud: Tunc ipse filius subjicietur*, PG 44.1317, as quoted in Emil Mersch, S.J., *The Whole Christ* (Ex Fontibus Company [1938] 2018), p. 318.

having become one with us in all things, he makes his
own all that is ours. But the greatest of all our goods is
surrender to God, which brings all creation into harmony. . . . Thus all creation becomes one body, all are
grafted one upon the other.[80]

The elements for the deification of the cosmos are all at
play here, perhaps reflecting Gregory of Nyssa's profound
appreciation for the works of Origen. As perhaps the first
"mystical theologian" of all the Church's trusted theologians, Gregory saw how the Incarnation changed not only
human nature but all material creation. If God has taken on
the very elements from which our bodies are made, if God
has assumed the very soul that informs our bodies, there is
no level of creation not brilliantly affected by God's descent
into his own good creation.

While the brothers Gregory and Basil standout as
trustworthy and wise Churchmen leading dioceses and
monasteries and congregations in the ongoing explication of central Christian mysteries, their friend Gregory of
Nazianzus displayed a much quieter and introspective manner. It was perhaps this stillness and interiority that allowed
Nazianzen to produce such an unmatchable collection of
poems and theological orations, the multi-layeredness of
which still produces fruit today.

One distinguishing mark of Gregory's theology is
his ongoing concern about the heresy of Apollinarianism, named after its founder Apollinaris of Laodicea (d.
390). Apollinarianism taught that while the incarnate Son

---

80   Ibid., 319 (PG 4041317-20).

of God was truly clothed with a human body, his divine Logos replaced any human mind or created faculty of cogitation. Nazianzen, therefore, countered by accentuating, whenever he talked about Jesus Christ, the Messiah's conformity to the whole of the human condition, body and soul. If Christ did not possess a truly human mind with all its wonderful abilities, how could we call him truly human? In Gregory's way of countering Apollinarianism, the humility of divine love shines wonderfully forth:

> And becoming man, God on earth, because his human nature was united to God, and became one person because the higher nature prevailed *in order that I too might be made God so far as he is made man.* He was born—but he had been (eternally) begotten; he was born (in time) of a woman—but she was a virgin. The first is human; the second divine. In his human nature he had no father; but also in his divine nature no mother. Both these belong to the Godhead. He dwelt in the womb—and he was recognized by [John] the prophet, himself still in the womb, leaping before the Word, for whose sake he came into being (Lk 1:41). He was wrapped in swaddling clothes— but he took off the swathing bands of the grave by his rising again. He was laid in a manger—but he was glorified by the angels, and proclaimed by a star, and worshiped by the Magi.[81]

---

[81]   Gregory Nazianzen, *Theological Oration* 3.19; Hardy, *op. cit.*, 173–74; slightly adjusted, and emphasis mine.

Tracing these various stages of existence, Gregory is deeply aware how "for that which he has not assumed he has not healed; but that which is united to his Godhead is also saved."[82]

The unquestionable commonality between Christ's human nature (*ousia*) and the rest of humankind was thus stressed by Gregory, because he knew this common nexus was the key both to God's true incarnation as well as our divinization. The Greek play on words made this link even more poetic: in the Son of God's *kenosis* is our *theosis*. That is, in the Son of God's emptying himself to become human (Phil 2:7) is our being able to be filled up by his divinity. "O the paradoxical blending! He who is comes into being, and the uncreated is created, and the uncontained is contained. . . . The one who enriches becomes poor; he is made poor in my flesh, that I might be enriched through his divinity. The full one empties himself; for he empties himself of his own glory for a short time, that I may participate in his fullness."[83] The Cappadocians thus stand at the end of the Trinitarian controversies and at the beginning of the Christological concerns of the fifth century. Their lasting legacy will be that they helped the Church finalize the language she would employ to best describe the Trinity, influencing our theological doctrines and religious disciplines even still.

In stressing how God is to be understood as one nature and three persons, the Cappadocians uncovered an amazing

---

[82] *ep.* 101; Hardy, *op. cit.*, 218.

[83] Gregory of Nazianzus, Oration 38.13, trans. Nonna Verna Harrison, *Festal Orations: St. Gregory of Nazianzus* (Crestwood, N.Y.: St. Vladimir's Seminary Press, 2008), 71.

truth: each person of the Trinity is 100 percent reliant upon another to be who he is. Unlike you and I who have our own autonomous humanity—my father is deceased but I remain; you and I have all had friends and relationships come in and out of our lives, yet we continue to be essentially who we are—the persons of the Trinity do not have their own separate divinity, but all share one and the same nature. Yet as distinct persons, the Father and the Son and the Holy Spirit differ not in what they are, but only in who they are: their relationships therefore define them wholly. You and I are only partially defined by relationships, but the Father is wholly dependent upon the Son to be the Father, and the Son is wholly and completely dependent upon the Father to be the Son, and the Spirit is entirely dependent upon their relationship for him to have his identity as the union or the gift between the Father and the Son, the love between the Lover and the Beloved.

Stressing the perfect union of the Father and Son and Spirit led the Cappadocians to describe the Trinity as a great dance, what Gregory Nazianzen first called the *Perichoresis* of God—literally, the dancing around—or the perfectly harmonious interaction between Father and Son and Holy Spirit. The Father gives himself wholly over to the Son and in the Son's accepting of the Father, the Holy Spirit is realized as the mutual giving and given-ness of each. This was the Cappadocian way of describing what they understood Christ to be saying in his high priestly prayer, asking the Father that all may be one as he and the Father are one, "I in you and you in me" (Jn 17:21). The Cappadocians strove to capture the mystery of the Trinity using terminology and phrasing which plumbed the depths of the doctrine without ever exhausting them, showing how the Son and the Holy Spirit are both fully God, yet different persons with their own distinctive operations within the Trinity as well as within salvation history.

From the writings of Basil, Gregory Nazianzen, and Gregory of Nyssa, then, we can see the importance of relationship. They stressed that God is, above all, a relationship of persons who are so entirely loving that they long to give themselves to the other. And whereas earlier theologians stressed this interdependence between Father and Son, it was left to the Cappadocians to unfold the importance of the Holy Spirit in the completion and perfection of this unity. Their labors would be ratified at the Church's next ecumenical council, and so we now turn to the effect they had in the official records of the First Council of Constantinople in 381.

The First Council of Constantinople

We saw at this chapter's outset that the Council of Nicaea was called to unify the Church around one acceptable Trinitarian creed. The major concern there in 325 was the consubstantiality between the Father and the Son, while the role of the Holy Spirit was left with a simple, "I believe in the Holy Spirit." There was nothing more that was professed about the Spirit in the Nicene Symbol. However, under the guidance of the Cappadocians, the bishops convened at the Council of Constantinople over the early summer months in 381 realized a fuller profession was needed and so wrote and included the clause that was incorporated into the Creed we say today.

Why was the addition needed? Back in the year 342, Constantinople had welcomed a new bishop, Macedonius, an efficient and worldly man who was adept at securing the proper political backing needed for his ecclesial security. Taking advantage of the tensions between Nicenes and anti-Nicene officials, Macedonius was able to advance his anti-Holy Spirit theology as well as viciously persecute anyone who opposed his vision for the Church. The theology which became associated with his name, Macedonianism, was an extreme Arian movement which relegated the Holy Spirit to a lesser type of divinity. Later known by the epithet "Pneumatomachianism"—literally, "Those who fight against the spirit"—it was a simplistic hodgepodge of ethereal abstractions relegating the Son to a creature merely similar (*homoiousios*) to the Father, while the Spirit was a further subordinate creation of the Son.

By 374, it became clear that subordinationism had made its way onto the world stage; it was denounced by Pope Damasus in Rome. Those concerned about Church unity thus began to make arrangements for another ecumenical council in order to address both the faulty thinking of the Pneumatomachi and to answer the many questions which had arisen since the time of Nicaea. By 381, then, Theodosius called to Constantinople all the recognized bishops of the empire. Approximately 150 bishops in all came and sought to reestablish ecclesial unity and to stave off any dissent. The first major task upon convening was to depose Maximus, who had sought the episcopal see of

Constantinople illegitimately and to install instead Gregory of Nazianzus. Gregory was thereupon consecrated but
was opposed by those Pneumatomachi who arrived late and
were not able to vote. But these Spirit-fighters also had a
more serious claim: according to Canon 15 of the Council
of Nicaea which read that "neither bishop, presbyter, nor
deacon shall pass from city to city," Gregory should not
have abandoned the people at Sasima for the great city of
Constantinople. Given his mild temperament, Gregory
recused himself and withdrew from consideration: "Let me
be as the Prophet Jonah! I may have caused this storm, but
for the salvation of this ship, I would gladly sacrifice myself.
But you, seize me and toss me into the ocean. . . . For I was
never happy when I ascended the cathedra here, and am all
too glad to come down off it."[84]

Eventually the proceedings got underway and it was
determined that the only way the Pneumatomachi could
be sufficiently condemned was to elaborate on what the
Nicene Creed had asserted so simply about the Holy Spirit.
After prayer and deliberation, therefore, it was agreed upon
that the Christian profession in the Holy Spirit would be
expanded from "I believe in the Holy Spirit" to "I believe in
the Holy Spirit, the Giver of Life, who proceeds from the
Father, who with the Father and the Son is equally worshipped and glorified, who has spoken through prophets."
The Holy Spirit is the object of Christian devotion and
worship, One who comes from the Father and has been at
work since the foundation of the earth. But he is not here
called God, and in fact, even in his monumental work *On*

---

[84]   Gregory of Nazianzus, *Autobiographical Poems* 2.1828-55; *Patrologia Graeca* 37.1157–9, my translation.

the Holy Spirit quoted above, Basil the Great avoids calling the Holy Spirit "God/*Theos*" altogether as well. Perhaps
those present at First Constantinople were content letting
the Holy Spirit be "equally worshiped and glorified," assur-
ing the faithful that this was obviously a quality of God
alone. Perhaps this insistence without actually calling the
Holy Spirit "God" was a capitulation to the strong Arian-
izing tendencies of many of the eastern bishops, placating
another possible threat of schism and ongoing division.

Another surprising move at First Constantinople was
the addition of one's belief and trust not only in the Father
and Son and Holy Spirit, but also in their Church. What
was never discussed at the Council of Nicaea now became
an official tenet of faith: "I believe in one, holy, catholic and
apostolic Church. I confess one baptism for the forgiveness
of sins and I look forward to the resurrection of the dead
and the life of the world to come. Amen." This final clause
assured assent not only to the Trinitarian dogma worked
out between 325 and 381 but also to any official Church
teaching thereafter. This final clause of the Creed thus com-
mits the baptized to putting their trust in the Church as
no mere human invention or institution but as a divinely
supported body whose truth claims are safeguarded by the
Holy Spirit himself. Like the incarnate Son, the Church is
both human and divine: divine, or else we would not place
our theological gift of faith in her; human, in that she is
lived out through the fallible and oftentimes scandalous
actions of imperfect persons.

As a result of First Constantinople, the creed
Christians profess today is more accurately the

Nicene-Constantinopolitan Creed. As a result of this gathering, Theodosius suppressed the Pneumatomachi, the theology of the Cappadocians was ratified as orthodox and trustworthy, so that what could be called the "Cappadocian Settlement" laid the groundwork for future Trinitarian speculation. This "Cappadocian Settlement" succinctly and accurately illuminated the aim of Nicaea, elucidating the mystery of the Trinitarian God as *mia ousia, tres hypostases*—one substance, three persons. This formula allowed later thinkers to affirm the consubstantiality of all three divine persons.

But those who profess the Creed today may have noticed one glaring omission from the Nicene-Constantinopolitan Creed. For most Christians in the West today profess belief in the Holy Spirit who "proceeds from the Father and the Son." This later addition, "and the Son," is known as the *Filioque*. This clause became a major source of division between East and West in the early Middle Ages and is still invoked to this day as a primary cause of the Great Schism of 1054. But what led to this dogmatic development? What is also known as a "double procession" theology, the *Filioque* was adopted in order to combat the perseverance of Arian tendencies across the empire. In those places where subordinating the divine persons was still active, it seemed right to counter by emphasizing how the Spirit is intrinsically related to both Father *and to the Son*. Many lines from the Cappadocian authors support this view that the Holy Spirit processes from the Father and the Son as their eternal union of Love, yet other lines from these same seminal authors insist that the Spirit proceeds directly from the

Father alone. As we shall see, the key Trinitarian thinkers of the West like Hilary and Augustine are more than insistent that the *Filioque* and a double procession Trinitarianism is the most fitting manner of understanding the Spirit's eternal origin.

Consequently, by the time Gothic Arians encountered authentic Catholic Christianity, the *Filioque* was seen as a necessary means of evangelization. That is why the Council of Toledo in 589, which proved so important in reuniting Arians of all sorts with the Church, became the first official ecclesial gathering to insert this article into the Nicene-Constantinopolitan Creed. In fact, it was Emperor Charlemagne's (d. 814) insistent pressing of Pope Hadrian (d. 795) that allowed the clause to be maintained permanently in the chanted creeds of the West, spreading the *Filioque* throughout the West as a sign of ecclesial fidelity. The Frankish monks in Jerusalem introduced the *Filioque* around 807, heightening the already existing tensions between Greek and Latin clergy. Emperor Charlemagne was incensed that patriarchs and metropolitans of the East were able to be installed into office without professing faith in the Spirit's procession from the Son. In response, he drew up the *Libri Carolini* which cemented the *Filioque* throughout the Carolingian Empire of the early Middle Ages. Thereafter, local synods and regional councils of bishops more and more insisted on the *Filioque*. In 1014 in Rome, Pope Benedict VII (who owed the success of his papacy to King Henry II of Germany, a strong advocate of the *Filioque* clause) irrevocably inserted the "and from the Son" into the creed forever.

Conclusion

Following the example of the first-century apostles in Acts 15, who came together to discuss the conversion of Gentiles, fourth-century apostles met in Nicaea to settle the pressing question of whether the Son of God was truly God or a lesser form of divinity. The answer formulated and "codified" at that council is on the lips and in the hearts of all Christians today: "God from God, light from light, true God from true God, consubstantial (*homoousios*) with the Father." By the end of the fourth century, that same reasoning would be applied by the Cappadocians to the person of the Holy Spirit. Pneumatology, the study of the person of the Holy Spirit (*Pneuma* in Greek), came to a crisis point in the mid-fourth century when a group arose around Bishop Macedonius of Constantinople known as the Pneumatomachi, who wrongly claimed that the Spirit was not a separate divine person. Into this debate arose the "Cappadocian Settlement," in which the Cappadocian Fathers explained the Trinity as "one substance yet three divine persons."

The fourth century was a boisterous but blessed era in the Church's history. Christians began those hundred years as a minority, persecuted bloodily and boldly by Diocletian and his minions, but their Faith was legalized under Constantine in 313. Shortly thereafter, doctrinal divisions arose. We begin the Lord's Prayer by praying to a communal Father, "Our Father," clearly stressing how charity and unity are important. Hence, as one would expect, not only does the sin—i.e., failures of charity—present in all the Church's faithful constantly threaten that desired harmony, so, too, do theological and creedal divisions. The first major imperial threat to ecclesial unity was Arianism, a simplistic anti-Trinitarian proposal that attempted to safeguard the one true God from polytheism by robbing the Son of God of his true divinity through the language of subordination. In the maelstrom which ensued, God raised up saints to combat any deviance from the teachings the Lord himself imparted to fallible men. Athanasius of Alexandria was raised up by God as one of the Church's great defenders. Even after decades of exile and calumny, the Athanasian vision of the Trinity emerged victorious.

When the same subordinating tendencies were applied to the Holy Spirit, imagining him as a sort of superior creature, God raised up a new generation of saints in the Cappadocian Fathers: Basil the Great, Gregory of Nyssa, and their friend Gregory Nazianzen. These three inspired not only correct doctrine but proper Christian fidelity and devotion. Basil even founded the first hospital as we think of it today (originally called a *Basileias* after him, these homes of benevolence and healing were condemned by pagan officials as unnecessarily scandalous and risky to the health of others). By the end of the fourth century, it was quite clear that Catholicism would stand as the prevailing culture of both the East and the West. God had become a man, had founded a Church, and he continues to labor to instill his life into all who wish to think and act like him. He became human so we could become divinized.

In closing this chapter and leading into our next, we may point out the obvious fact that when God became man, he came to the world as we all do, as a little child with a human mother. If it is humbling to think of this process of deification of becoming godly, it is equally so to think how God humbled himself by becoming one of us. It is perhaps even more awesome to consider that the entire work of salvation which God achieved through the incarnation of his Son was realized only because one creature, one woman, one of us freely said yes to the Father and offered herself to the Spirit's fruitful overshadowing. Mary is the humble bridge between heaven and earth, the one who surrenders fully to God, both body and soul, from her very first moment of existence. In so doing, Mary becomes not only the mother of Jesus Christ, she mystically becomes the mother of all her Christian children in the order of divine grace. How this adoption came to be understood and how it came to be expressed theologically is the topic of our next chapter. Even though we shall now move westward to the great Latin Fathers of the Church, this devotion to the mystery of Mary's assent has never been absent from the Greek-speakers, who did so much to lay the foundations of Christian thought. Accordingly, we conclude with a sagacious warning from Gregory of Nazianzus: "Whoever does not accept Holy Mary as the Mother of God has no relation with the Godhead. Whoever says that he was channeled, as it were, through the Virgin but not formed directly with her divinely and humanly ("divinely" because without a husband, "humanly" because by law of conception) is likewise godless."[85]

---

[85]   Gregory of Nazianzus, *The First Letter to Cledonius the Presbyter* (*epistle* 101, around 382), trans. Wickham, *On God and Christ, op. cit.*, p. 156.

Hail, Full of Grace

MARY, MOTHER OF THE CHURCH AND EPHESUS (431)

"And he came to her and said, 'Hail, full of grace, the Lord is with you!' But she was greatly troubled at the saying, and considered in her mind what sort of greeting this might be. And the angel said to her, 'Do not be afraid, Mary, for you have found favor with God. And behold, you will conceive in your womb and bear a son, and you shall call his name Jesus'" (Lk 1:28–31).

DOES BEING "FULL of grace" mean that there is no room for anything that is not grace? No disobedience, no self-centeredness, no sin? The Mariology of the early Church was as powerful as it was poetic: theologians and hymnists dedicated large amounts of time and material to understanding and honoring this woman who united heaven and earth. She was depicted as the "neck" between the divine Head and his earthly Body.

So far we have seen how, for the early centuries, Christian life was "lived" in Greek, and most of the significant events occurred mainly in oriental lands. But beginning with the North African Tertullian (d. c. 240) whom we met in chapter 2, the Latin world began to provide powerful theological speculation and sanctifying pastoral practicality. We have also seen how Nicaea answered the relationship between the Son and the Father in 325 and how the Spirit's own unique divinity was addressed at the First Council of Constantinople in 381. So, whereas the East was occupied with addressing the nature and relationships of the divine persons within the Trinity, it seems that most of the energy in the West was spent addressing the nature and relationships among persons in the Church.

This chapter will continue chronologically and highlight the important theologians of the patristic West, working our way up to the Council of Ephesus in 431, the third ecumenical council, and the one at which Mary's title as the "Mother of God" was officially ratified. At Ephesus, the conciliar theology of how God's humanity in Christ was related to the humanity he came to save began to be worked out. As we make our way to Ephesus, this chapter focuses on three Latin theologians whose influence on the history of Christian thought is difficult to overstate. The first is St. Jerome, whose translation of the Sacred Scriptures from Hebrew and Greek into Latin opened the Bible for the simplest of readers. The next figure we treat is St. Ambrose of Milan, former soldier turned bishop, whose work for ecclesial unity in the heart of the imperial capital helped keep the Church unified in very tense times. The third section focuses on St. Augustine, who is arguably the most important Christian thinker after St. Paul. Having examined the great contributions of these late fourth- and early fifth-century theologians, this chapter concludes with the Council of Ephesus in 431, which confirmed the Christian people's desire to invoke Mary as the Mother of God, a truly special devotion for the woman whose yes allowed God to enter his own good creation.

As we trace the major figures and themes of the first five hundred years of Christ's Church, it is essential to focus on Mary because it is she who allows God and humanity to become one. It is Mary's *fiat mihi secundum verbum tuum*, "let it be to me according to your word" (Lk 1:38), that gave the Almighty license to descend into his own creation. For the early Christians, Marian devotion served as more than just another pious practice; it was an essential part of understanding how God works and what God desires for those made in his image and likeness. A real-life flesh-and-blood woman from a particular time and place guaranteed the Savior's true humanity; her youthful virginity safeguarded his divine paternity. The Christ who comes to save humanity is thus born twice, eternally as divine and in time as man. Or, as St. Augustine put it one Christmas morning, "Born of his mother, he commended this day to the ages, while born of his Father he created all ages. That birth could have no mother, while this one required no man as father. To sum up, Christ was born both of a Father and of a mother; both without a father and without a mother; of a Father as God, of a mother as man; without a mother as God, without a father as man."[86] Here, in this woman,

---

[86]   Augustine, *sermon* 184.3; trans. Edmund Hill, O.P., *Sermons* III/6 (Hyde Park, NY: New City Press, 1993), p. 18; to date, this series of the *Works of Saint Augustine: A Translation for the 21ˢᵗ Century* is the best collection of all of Augustine of Hippo's works in English.

in this womb, in this yes, the Great Exchange of God's
humanity for our divinization is effected. God is now able
to personally dwell in those whom he has loved from afar
for so long. As we now treat the significance of Jerome,
Ambrose, and Augustine, we shall pay special attention to
how these fifth-century Latin Fathers understood the role
of Mary in their most significant theological works.

St. Jerome (c. 342-420)

From his own reflections, we know something of the earliest
origins of Eusebius Hieronymus. Born sometime around
345 in ancient Stridon, in what is today either Croatia or
Slovakia, Jerome received the best of an elite education in
Rome, showing an uncanny ability to reproduce the rhetorical flares and flourishes of the best of the Latin masters,
Cicero and Virgil especially. Here in Rome, he converted
at around the age of nineteen and was baptized into the
Catholic faith. As a young adult he became instantly enam-
ored with the texts of the Faith and was inspired to travel
in order to experience the Christian life more deeply at
important sites. He went first to Trier in Gaul and there
encountered the writings of Bishop Hilary of Poitiers and
grew infatuated with what he read of the heroic virtue and
piety of the desert monks in the East. Such admiration
moved him to make a pilgrimage throughout Asia Minor
and Syria, where he fell in love with the monastic life. While
living a life of extreme asceticism and study in the Desert of
Chalcis (south of modern-day Aleppo), Jerome refined his

knowledge of Greek and began his Hebrew tutorials from a local Jewish convert.

It was during this time that Jerome experienced his famous dream. One night in 378 or 379, Jerome awoke with a start. Priding himself on his fluency in so many languages, Jerome saw himself overconfidently appear before the Lord Jesus for final judgment, assuming he would be lavished with many honors befitting one so intelligent. It was a shock for Jerome to realize that when God spoke, he let him know in no uncertain terms, *Ciceronianus es, non Christianus*—"Thou art a Ciceronian, not a Christian. *Where thy treasure is, there is thy heart also.* I was struck dumb on the spot."[87] Jerome henceforth promised never to put the importance of classical literature over and against the Christian Scriptures, an oath which he never really embraced and which only gave his enemies ammunition against the proud grammarian.

Try as he may, Jerome was really never able to offer up his love of letters. After living this ascetic life for some time, he returned to the Metropolis of Antioch and was ordained a priest there just before 380, at which time he left for further study in Constantinople under Gregory Nazianzen. Later, by then widely known for possessing a most agile and gifted mind, he was enrolled as the Vatican secretary in Rome and served Pope Damasus there from 382–85. Here Jerome consecrated his love of languages by producing the most famous fruit of his labors: a new translation of the

---

[87] Jerome to Eustochium, *epistle* 22.30; *The Letters of St. Jerome*, trans. Thomas Comerford Lawler (Westminster, MD: The Newman Press), p. 166.

entire Bible, from both the Hebrew and Greek originals, into readable, lowly or "vulgar" Latin, hence known today as the Vulgate. In Rome, Jerome continued his Hebrew tutorials with a local rabbi and led Christian study groups of aristocratic women who would come to fund his later travels back to the deserts of the East

When Siricius was elected bishop of Rome in 384, Jerome departed the eternal city under a cloud, stirred up by some invidious enemies who spread ugly rumors about his friendship with his wealthy women friends, particularly his relationship with an older widow Paula and her two daughters, Blaesilla and Eustochium, whom he met in the summer of 382. The friendship was cause for some comment as some pharisaical and influential prudes doubted an ascetic priest and a holy widow could enjoy a chaste friendship. In addition, once the more worldly daughter of the two, Blaesilla renounced that life after having survived an almost fatal sickness; she zealously embraced Jerome's level of asceticism but died after only a few months of this regiment. Burdened with this sorrow and innuendo, Jerome moved permanently back to the Holy Land with Paula and Eustochium. There, Paula donated enough of her resources to found two monasteries (and continued to lavish such generosity that at one point she actually found herself in debt). Never having left behind her business prowess, Paula regained her losses and continued to serve as Jerome's patroness, enabling him to produce some of his most important scriptural commentaries and theological works during this time.

Despite being at the service of the pope for only three years—and despite his estimation of the Roman clergy as

the "Senate of the Pharisees"—Jerome never lost his awareness that Rome was the place where Peter the Rock offered
the guarantee of one's following Christ. Here, the Church
proved to be the ship of safety (that is why the central part
of a Catholic church is called the "nave," from the Latin
for ship, *navis*) against the tumult of the world. The Vicar
of Christ, the bishop of Rome, offered the surest and most
direct access to the mind and heart of the Savior, and that
is why St. Jerome once wrote Pope Damasus to thank him.

> My words are spoken to the successor of the fisher-
> man, to the disciple of the cross. As I follow no leader
> save Christ, so I communicate with none but your
> blessedness, that is with the Chair of Peter. For this, I
> know, is the rock on which the Church is built! This is
> the house where alone the paschal lamb can be rightly
> eaten. This is the ark of Noah, and he who is not found
> in it shall perish when the flood prevails. But since by
> reason of my sins I have betaken myself to this desert
> which lies between Syria and the uncivilized waste,
> I cannot, owing to the great distance between us,
> always ask of your sanctity the holy thing of the Lord.
> Consequently I here follow the Egyptian confessors
> who share your faith, and anchor my frail craft under
> the shadow of their great argosies. I know nothing of
> Vitalis; I reject Meletius; I have nothing to do with
> Paulinus. He that gathers not with you scatters; he
> that is not of Christ is of Antichrist.[88]

---

[88] Jerome to Damasus, *epistle* 15.2; trans. W. H. Fremanle, *Nicene and Post-Nicene Fathers*, op. cit., vol. 6, pp. 18–19. Here Jerome separates

It is the Apostle Peter and not one of the *nouveau* heretics
who brings us closer to Christ, and this closeness results in
Christ's pouring his life into those opening up to him. There
is an identity forged between Christ and Christian which
enjoys a magisterial charism in the successors of Peter.

While our theme of Christ's life becoming one with
each of our lives is not central to Jerome, whose passion
and duties forced his mind to dwell instead on matters of
Scripture and doctrine, he can easily say that this deifying
transformation is precisely why the Word became flesh and
why that enfleshed God founded a Church before ascending back to the Father: "The Word was made flesh that we
might pass from the flesh into the Word. The Word did not
cease to be what he had been; nor did the human nature
lose that which it was by birth. The glory was increased, the
nature was not changed."[89] In his taking on of human flesh,
the Word foregoes no divinity but assumes all of humanity to himself. In his humanity, then, the incarnate Son
increases God's glory by transforming sinners into saints.

The writings of Jerome were hugely influential in
promoting study and sustained reflection on the Sacred
Scriptures, but also very important were his writings on
consecrated virginity. Regarding Scripture, he is most

---

himself from three late fourth-century heretics: Vitalis (d. c. 400)
who erred in his Christology, following Apollinaris's lead in thinking
Christ did not need a human psyche, Meletius (d. 381), a schismatic
whose Arian leanings made him suspicious and divided the Church in
Antioch, and Paulinus, who reacted so strongly against Arianism that
he seemed to fall into a sort of Monarchianism, earning the ire of St.
Basil.

[89]   *Against Jovinianus* 2.29, trans. W. H. Fremantle, *Nicene and Post-Nicene Fathers*, op. cit., vol. 6, p. 410.

significant for his translations and his in-depth commentaries. His approach to Scripture could be described as particularly energetic. For Jerome, it was a matter not simply of engaging a text but encountering the living Word: "For if, as Paul says, Christ is the power of God and the wisdom of God, and if the man who does not know Scripture does not know the power and wisdom of God, then ignorance of Scripture is ignorance of Christ."[90] Also from his time in the Holy Land came his commentaries on Paul, on Ecclesiastes, on the Psalms, Genesis, on the Gospel of Matthew, as well as on parts of the Gospel of Luke, John's Prologue as well as select scenes from Revelation. Jerome's cataloging of significant Christian writers (*De uiris illustribus*) also helped form a canon of trustworthy theologians for posterity to safely draw upon and trust for the ongoing task of expounding sacred doctrine.

Jerome's writings also proved hugely important in the early Church for his upholding of Christian chastity. We first meet this theme in his widely-read letters to Eustochium. Most important in antiquity were *Epistle* 22 on the purpose and duties of virginity, as opposed to the vile lewdness of ancient Rome, and his classic *Epistle* 108 which is meant as a comfort for Eustochium after her mother's death in 404. It is the fulfilment of a promise Jerome made to take care of these vulnerable women, and he opens the letter by admitting, "If all the members of my body were to be converted into tongues, and if each of my limbs were

---

[90] Jerome's *Preface* to his *Commentary on Isaiah*,; trans. Thomas Scheck, vol. 68 in the Ancient Christian Writers Series (New York: Newman Press, 2015), p. 67.

to be gifted with a human voice, I could still do no justice to the virtues of the holy and venerable Paula." In a much more polemic tone, we have his works against Helvidius and Jovinian who denied Mary's virginity. This is also where we read Jerome's Mariology, a beautiful example of fourth-century Latin devotion, which serves as a sort of signpost for us as we make our way toward the Council of Ephesus.

It should not surprise us that Jerome's concerns about Mary typically take place in his defense of virginity. After all, it was in the context of the monastic life and the asceticism he himself fostered in his cave in Bethlehem that Jerome's study of Mary blossomed. Jerome seemed to have an argumentative spirit and never backed away from a fight. He combatted the errors of Origen, the self-sufficiencies of the Pelagians, and especially the corrupt teachings of Helvidius and Jovinian. These two belonged to a movement sprouting up in late antique Christianity which placed marriage on the same par, if not above, consecrated virginity. Using Mary as the perfect model of both of these holy vocations in life, Jerome the monk (and cantankerous celibate, to be honest) felt called to defend a pious belief in the Church that since Jesus and Our Lady both chose not to enter into the sacrament of Holy Matrimony, virginity retained an objectively higher level of holiness in the Church.

In so doing, Jerome opened up for posterity the correct way of reading Scripture when it came to the Annunciation, Mary's relationship with Joseph, and the virginal life itself. Mary is the new Ark of the Covenant, the first living Tabernacle whose very body houses the Savior of the world, and those around her must show the proper reverence. Jerome therefore challenges his opponent on the glory of virginity to make his point, "Helvidius, I say, would have us believe that Joseph, well acquainted with such surprising wonders, dared to touch the temple of God, the abode of the Holy Ghost, the mother of his Lord?"[91] Throughout his treatise, Jerome is insistent that Mary remained a virgin before, after, and even during the birth of Jesus Christ, not knowing the curse of physical rupture promised to the fallen Eve as she was being cast out from Paradise (Gn 3:16).[92]

Jerome has been held up as one of the four Latin Doctors of the Church alongside Ambrose, Augustine, and Gregory the Great. While he lacked the political import of the bishop of Milan, the theological depth of the bishop of Hippo, and the ecclesial significance of the bishop of Rome, Jerome is still hailed as a foremost biblical theologian whose work on the Sacred Scriptures helped the Church come to understand how the Holy Spirit speaks to the Church through these divinely inspired pages. In his writings, there is a certain stress on the need for unity between Christ and Christian, but it is muted and is often glossed over for the sake of other issues dear to Jerome's mind and heart.

Jerome died on September 30, 420, the day that now marks his feast. He breathed his last in Bethlehem, but his remains were later translated to the great basilica of Maria Maggiore in Rome in order to be near the true crib

---

[91] *On Perpetual Virginity* §8; trans. Fremantle, *Nicene and Post-Nicene Fathers, op. cit.,* vol. 6, p. 338.

[92] Jerome sees the birth of Christ through the intact body of Mary as a foreshadowing of his divine ability to walk through locked doors without any impairment; see his *Commentary on John* 1.1–14.

of Christ housed there. This is a fitting symbol marking Jerome's love of Rome and his love of the Blessed Mother who gave birth to the Savior of all humankind. Although the office of cardinal is a later development, as secretary to the Holy Father, Jerome is usually depicted with a cardinal's red hat (the *galero*) and he is also typically depicted with a lion, imagery which comes from a legend that, when he lived in the desert, Jerome once healed a lion's paw.

St. Ambrose

If a lion and a cardinal's hat are symbols of St. Jerome, a beehive represents the great bishop of Milan. Legend has it that when Ambrose was still only a child in the crib, a clustering of bees formed around his mouth with the most gentle of buzzing, indicating that this young boy would one day be a mellifluous orator. While Ambrose is perhaps most famous for his discipling the great Augustine into the fullness of Christ's Church, his own story is worth knowing as well. Ambrose (c. 340–397) was a successful man of the world like Augustine but one who was overcome by grace and who had left career, family, and worldliness behind in order to pursue Christ more single-heartedly.

We know from various sources that Ambrose was born into a Roman aristocratic family somewhere in Gallica Belgica (where today Luxembourg, France, and Belgium would intersect), most probably in Trier where his father was a Gallican praetorian prefect, a sort of high-ranking political advisor. Ambrose's mother came from one of the oldest and certainly wealthiest families of Rome (the *Aurelii*

Symmachi), and he thus received the finest Roman education possible, his family moving to the eternal city after his father's early death when Ambrose was a young teenager. A distinguished person in Roman circles, Ambrose attracted the attention of the aristocratic class which enlisted him into public service. By 372, he had been made governor of the rich Milanese provinces of Emilia and Liguria. During his short stint as governor (372–374) Ambrose won the respect of the citizenry and manifested excellent civil and political skill in caring for the common good.

As we saw earlier, Arianism was not eradicated by either of the first two ecumenical councils, and as late as 374, it still had its own powerful bishop in Milan. When the Arian bishop Auxentius died (about whom Athanasius once quipped that he was not only ignorant of Latin but was "totally unskilled in everything but impiety!"), Ambrose traveled to Milan to squelch rumors that a violent uprising was going to take place unless the Arians received the bishop they demanded. When Ambrose appeared and began to speak respectfully to both sides, a common roar went up demanding that Ambrose become bishop for all—a governor whose past has been sympathetic to Nicene Catholics but whose capacity for benevolence spread far and wide and was thus acceptable to the Arians who believed they could win him over. Unfortunately, a major obstacle stood in the way of this plan: Ambrose not only lacked any theological formation, he was not yet even baptized. After some time of prayer and discernment, he gave himself up for Baptism in Milan, was ordained into Holy Orders, and consecrated bishop of Milan (I tease my Jesuit brothers that within a week, St. Ambrose accomplished what we need thirteen years to do).

In cooperation with the pro-Nicene Emperor Gratian, Ambrose straightaway instituted laws against paganism and worked for unity in the Church of Jesus Christ where his gifts in administration shined forth. Ambrose thus became an instant disappointment—and enemy—of the Arian faction in Milan. Theologically, Ambrose explicated how Christ's life is to be lived out in his Church. He stressed 2 Peter 1:4 and our participation in the divine life alongside the biblical imagery of our being adopted as the Father's beloved sons and daughters. Although perhaps more of an administrator than a theologian, Ambrose was also given over to hours of prayer and study. While he was not as prolific as a Jerome or Augustine, his works are full of clear and satisfying explanations of creedal truths.

For example, in his work *De Fide*, a beautiful treatise written at the request of Emperor Gratian for his uncle Valens (an Arian sympathizer), Ambrose teaches in one masterful stroke that the pinnacle of the Christian life is a Church in whom Christ is alive in each, extending his sacrificial oblation to the Father in and through each of his believers:

> For He is the foundation of all, and is the head of the Church, in Whom our common nature according to the flesh has merited the right to the heavenly throne. For the flesh is honoured as having a share in Christ Who is God, and the nature of the whole human race is honoured as having a share in the flesh.

As we then sit in Him by fellowship in our fleshly nature, so also He, Who through the assumption of our flesh was made a curse for us (seeing that a curse could not fall upon the blessed Son of God), so, I say, He through the obedience of all will become subject in us; when the Gentile has believed, and the Jew has acknowledged Him Whom he crucified; when the Manichaean has worshipped Him, Whom he has not believed to have come in the flesh; when the Arian has confessed Him to be Almighty, Whom he has denied; when, lastly, the wisdom of God, His justice, peace, love, resurrection, is in all. Through His own works and through the manifold forms of virtues Christ will be in us in subjection to the Father. And when, with vice renounced and crime at an end, one spirit in the heart of all peoples has begun to cleave to God in all things, then will God be all and in all.[93]

Notice that the bishop uses any teachings on unity to decry heresy and promote Church unity. Such unity can occur because it is the same Christ living in each of the Church's members. In so doing, Christ offers the sacrifice of his life in and through each of us as well; through Christ's obedience, we too then become subject to the same Father. It is this sort of mutual indwelling that keeps any Christian from bragging about his or her own achievements, for any holiness is ultimately Christ's dwelling within the saint.

---

[93] Ambrose of Milan, *Of the Christian Faith*, Bk. 5, ch. 14 (end of §180 and start of §181); trans. de Romestin, *Nicene and Post-Nicene Fathers, op. cit.,* vol. 10, p. 307.

This is perhaps why Ambrose does not shy away from comparing the life of a faithful Christian to the life of an obedient divine messenger. The baptized become like the angels, not in that they lose their bodies, but in that they become divinely docile. Through the yes of Mary, the heavenly Word became flesh in order that those in the flesh can in turn become heavenly. Do not be surprised, Ambrose states, that if we were to see ourselves as we shall become fully in Christ in heaven, we might forget that we were ever creatures: "Let us not, then, be surprised if they are compared to the angels who are joined to the Lord of angels. Who, then, can deny that this mode of life has its source in heaven, which we don't easily find on earth, except since God descended into the members of an earthly body? Then a Virgin conceived, and the Word became flesh that flesh might become God."[94] The flesh becomes God only because God became flesh, and in so doing still pours out his life into anyone willing to surrender to the graces of baptism.

Ambrose displays a typical Latin approach to the question of salvation: it is no mere atonement but a sanctification in which the contrite sinner is more than forgiven or reconciled, he is elevated by the Son of God's own descent. In an exchange of natures, we receive from Christ what he has taken from us: by taking our humanity to himself, he offers us his own divinity, and while the first may be a true union—Jesus is truly and unqualifiedly human—our involvement in divinity is always participatory and contingent upon God's grace but is nonetheless still a real

---

[94]   Ambrose, *On Virginity* Bk. 1, ch. 3, §11; trans. de Romestin, *op. cit.*, p. 365.

participation in perfection. For Ambrose, then, salvation is our being lifted "beyond our nature" as we are empowered to live a more-than-human life in Christ.

Similar to Jerome, Ambrose is fervent in stressing Mary's role in making this great exchange a reality. He is also like Jerome in stressing Mary's virginity in the story of salvation as the most fitting way that God becomes human without any trace of sexual concupiscence or bodily affliction for the childbearing mother. "What birth according to the flesh could be more fitting for God than this one, in which the immaculate Son of God, even in assuming a body, should maintain the purity of an immaculate birth? Surely the sign of the divine event consists in his being born of a virgin, not from a woman."[95]

As we shall see when we examine the technicalities of the Council of Ephesus, it is important to notice how the Church Fathers describe Mary's role in allowing the Son of God to become human and thus send his divine life out into his Church. He is born of Mary not just from her; that is, he is the very substance of Mary who contributes to human salvation by offering the Savior our humanity. She is the new Eve who gives life not only to the Son of God but to all her children in him; she is not just a receptacle or a vehicle through whom God becomes human. She has a role to play in the most significant moment of human history: "The flesh of Christ did not come down from heaven,

---

[95]   Ambrose, Exposition of Luke 2.78; quoted in Luigi Gambero, *Mary and the Fathers of the Church: The Blessed Virgin Mary in Patristic Thought* (San Francisco: Ignatius Press, 1999), p. 192. This is the leading book today for collections of patristic quotes on the central role of Mary in Christian salvation.

because he assumed it from the virgin on earth."[96] Jesus Christ is not only consubstantial with his heavenly Father, he is also consubstantial with his earthly mother.

Ambrose thus appears as the first Christian writer to refer to Mary as the "type and image" of Christ's Church. Mary is the face of what all Christians are to become, the pattern of our own salvation as we, too, must offer the divine our human body and soul in which he continues his life of filial obedience and neighborly charity. This self-offering marked Ambrose's entire episcopacy, and he was held in high esteem by friends and foes alike. He was a bishop intent on Church order as well as reform, never one beholden to simple tradition. Augustine, for example, shared with his readers some advice Ambrose gave him about following local ecclesial customs and finding a certain flexibility in the local Christian community. Augustine recalls how Ambrose told him, "When I go to Rome, I fast on Saturday; when I am here (at Milan), I do not fast. So to whatever church you go, observe its custom if you do not want to be a scandal to anyone or anyone to be a scandal to you."[97] It is to this Augustine that we now turn, as he is perhaps the "thing" for which Ambrose is best remembered.

Once Augustine left his Milanese mentor in 387, Bishop Ambrose carried on working for Church unity against the Arian remnants. He paid particular attention to the imperial court to ensure those who led society were receiving

[96] Ambrose, *On the Sacraments* 6.4; Gambero, *op. cit.*, p. 195.
[97] Augustine's *Answers to the Questions of Januarius, epistle* 54, Bk. 1.1.3; trans. Roland Teske, S.J., *Letters* II/1, *op. cit,.* p. 211. From this exchange, we have received the phrase, "When in Rome, do as the Romans do."

the best Catholic formation, and his care for the emperor
Theodosius paid off in the revitalization of the Church in
and around Milan. On April 4, 397, Ambrose died and was
entombed in the church that bears his name still today.

Of all his achievements, it is perhaps a baptism for
which Ambrose is best-known. On the Easter Vigil of
387, one just like him—worldly, eloquent, and desirous
of more—approached the font and knelt before Ambrose.
The name of this young man was known throughout most
of the pagan world, but now it was to be chanted by the
Church: Aurelius Augustinus would receive the waters of
life through the hands of Ambrose, thereby embarking on a
life in the Church which still serves to shape and influence
how we think of the Triune God of Love and the enigmatic
depths of the human person. In fact, after the Apostle Paul,
Augustine is arguably the Christian most responsible for
helping the Church formulate her most central doctrines:
teachings on grace, the sacraments, the end times, and the
ways in which God works intimately within the human
soul.

St. Augustine

Born in Thagaste in modern-day Algeria in 354, Augustine chose the "scenic route" to sainthood. Always at the
top of his class, he excelled at rhetoric and oratory but
was consumed by the question of where evil came from.
Born to a pagan father and a Christian mother—Patrick
and the future St. Monica—Augustine found the writings
and teachings of Christianity pat and simplistic. He thus

turned from the Church in which he had been enrolled (but not baptized) and joined an oriental sect, the Manichaeans. Mani was a third-century Persian mystic whose movement was a form of Gnosticism, positing a good god in constant war with a co-equal evil deity, a struggle that gave to this world an inevitable admixture of good and evil.

In this dualism, Augustine was able to find an easy answer to the problem of evil—it is an inevitable result of a cosmic battle from which we cannot escape. Augustine also found a convenient excuse for his youthful dalliances and sins. If evil is unavoidable, one need not grow in virtue or strive to overcome one's shortcomings. How useful to an upstart success slowly being surrounded by more and more worldly opportunities. For after his studies of grammar and rhetoric, Augustine landed a teaching job in Carthage where he was instantly recognized as a true master. It was not long until he was recognized and received a teaching position in Rome. But even Rome could not hold him long, and he was soon made the court orator up at Milan where the Roman emperor had moved the imperial seat. His position there was as a sort of propaganda master for the waning Roman Empire, and it was Augustine's job to make the emperor and his policies look appealing to the public. Such a high–profile position afforded him access to all the political intrigue and sensual delights a good pagan could ever want.

But perhaps God had brought him to Milan for a very different purpose, and Augustine became aware of this as he looked back on his life: "You were snatching me away, using my lusts to put an end to them."[98] For in the illustrious senator turned servant we just met, Augustine had finally met his match. While in Milan, Augustine came to respect Ambrose enough to sneak into the cathedral and catch his homilies (arriving during the liturgical cycle when Ambrose happened to be preaching on the book of Genesis). Augustine also came into contact with an intellectual circle centered around a new philosophy, Neo-Platonism, and it was among them he discovered two essential truths. Through the writings of Neo-Platonism's founder Plotinus (d. 270), Augustine came to see (1) that God is pure, uncreated spirit with nothing material or spatial or separable about him and (2) that evil is not an active force separate from the good but can in fact be understood only as the lack of the good, a parasite which eats away at existence but itself is not something independent.

Coming to see Christianity as not only something reasonable for the first time in his life but something actually true, Augustine resigned from the imperial court and presented himself to Bishop Ambrose for baptism on April 24, 387. At the Easter Vigil, Augustine, his son Adeodatus, along with his best friend Alypius, were all consecrated in the holy waters and began a new life. Augustine returned to North Africa with the intention of beginning a monastic community, his mother Monica having died on the Italian coast at Ostia as they awaited voyage. Yet once again God had other plans. The bishop of Hippo Regius, a relatively small port town (today's Annaba in coastal Algeria),

---

[98] *Confessions* 5.8.15 as in *Augustine's Confessions,* ed. David Vincent Meconi, SJ (San Francisco: Ignatius Press, 2012), p. 116.

sought Augustine out and pleaded that the best way the orator and philosopher could serve the Church was not in monastic isolation but in priestly preaching. In 391, Augustine was ordained a priest, and by 395, he had been elevated to bishop. His preaching was so attractive and his insights into the Christian mysteries so illuminating that people rarely left him alone. He consequently spent most of his day adjudicating cases between Christians and settling disputes within his diocese, while he spent most of the night responding to letters and crafting doctrinal essays with the hope of settling some confusion or answering some theological question. By the time he died in Hippo in August of 430, his work came to tally over one hundred separate treatises, over three hundred letters, and about six hundred significant sermons, over 4.5 million words, significantly more than any other Church Father.

Throughout these writings we meet perhaps the first Christian existentialist in that Augustine wrestled deeply with the meaning of life and the ennui of temporality. He was a man of deep passion and looked for fulfillment all around him. He was unquiet, he was restless, he knew the depths of depravity but longed for the heights of heaven. That is why when most people think of Augustine, they rightly think of his *Confessions*, written between 397 and 401, which really served as Augustine's way of introducing himself as a new bishop in Africa. Furthermore, when most people think of the *Confessions*, they think of the celebrated opening: "Great are you, O Lord . . . and our heart is restless until it rests in you."[99] And this is ultimately what

---

[99]   "*Confessions* 1.1.1; Meconi, *op. cit.*, p. 3.

Augustine means by "confession"—not the sacrament of
Reconciliation, but that more primal searching of the created soul thirsting for final meaning. No earthly romance,
no career, no level of material success can comfort a heart
made in the image and likeness of Love himself.

And the hallmark of Augustine's theology is how everything revolves around this interaction between a God who
is paradoxically closer to the creature than he is to himself and a creature who is gloriously made to become one
with God but sadly finds other loves just as alluring, realizing that God was "more intimately present to me than
my innermost being and higher than the highest peak of
my spirit. But I stumbled upon that bold woman devoid of
prudence in Solomon's allegory; she was sitting outside on
her stool and inviting me: *Come and enjoy eating bread in
secret, and drink sweet, stolen water* (Prov 9:18). She seduced
me because she found me living outside, in my carnal eyes,
and ruminating within myself only on what I had devoured
through them."[100]

Augustine knew viscerally, and better than most, how
difficult it was to rid oneself of loving wrongly. When he
began to love Christ and therefore love all else in him, his
sins, his fallen loves, beckoned, "Do you mean to get rid
of us? Shall we never be your companions again . . . never
. . . never again. . . . Do you imagine you will be able to
live without us?"[101] Augustine realized how deeply torn he
was, torn between loving God first and loving God's creatures first, but he also realized the power of grace, of God

---

[100] *Conf* 3.6.11; Meconi, *op. cit.*, p. 61.
[101] *Conf.* 8.11.26; Meconi, *op. cit.*, pp. 221–22; slightly adjusted.

himself, dwelling within the soul, within the heart which he had made for himself.

When we turn to Augustine's theology of Christ's unfurling his life into his followers, we encounter some of the most provocative and satisfying lines in the whole of the great Christian Tradition. For Augustine, the "whole Christ" (a term he coined, the *totus Christus*) is not just Jesus now seated at the right hand of the Father but the entire Christ is Jesus as well as those whom Jesus loves. This is what love achieves and effects, the inseparable union between lover and beloved and this is precisely what the Church and the whole of the Christian story is: Christ and Christian, an inseparable union. This is how Augustine can preach and advise his congregants in Hippo: "Let us congratulate ourselves then and give thanks for having been made not only Christians but Christ."[102] This is the primary force of love for Augustine: love not only unites lover and beloved but love actually establishes an identity between the two parties. In this way, it is ultimately love which makes one a member of Christ's body. "And he himself also becomes a member by loving, and through love he comes to be in the structure of Christ's body, and there shall be one Christ loving himself."[103]

What a generous and merciful love our Savior shows the world when even he surrenders himself to the transformative nature of love. This is how even God "identified his

---

[102]   *Homilies on the Gospel of John* 21.8; trans. Edmund Hill, *Homilies on the Gospel of John* (I/12), *op. cit.*, p. 379.
[103]   *Homilies on the First Epistle of John* 10.3; trans. Boniface Ramsey, *Homilies on the First Epistle of John* (I/14), *op. cit.*, p. 148.

members with himself, just as he did when he said, *I was hungry and you fed me* (Mt 25:35), and as he identified us with himself when he called from heaven to the rampaging Saul who was persecuting God's holy people, *Saul, Saul, why are you persecuting me?* (Acts 9:4), though no one was laying a finger on Christ himself. . . . 'See yourself reflected in me,' Christ says."[104] This is the "whole Christ," the *totus Christus*, the realization that the Lord longs to identify himself with those he loves. Christ did not come to be adored from afar, to be flattered or fawned over, but in becoming one of us, he wants to make us like himself. This is a reality even more remarkable and astounding than seeing God himself be born. Augustine in fact opens one of his Christmas Day homilies by teaching his flock that "something much more unbelievable has been paid us in advance: in order to make gods of those who were merely human, one who was God made himself human."[105]

Known in later centuries for his insistence that everything is gift, Augustine's appellation "the Doctor of Grace" fits well because he holds that everything we give to the Lord he has first given us. We have nothing of our own to give God, and so he gives us everything first. That is why even our deification is first and foremost a divine act:

> To what hope the Lord has called us, what we now carry about with us, what we endure, what we look forward to, is well known. . . . We carry mortality

---

[104] *Expositions of the Psalms* 32, exposition 2.2; trans. Maria Boulding, *Expositions on the Psalms* III/15, op. cit., p. 393.
[105] *Sermon* 192.1; trans. Hill, *Sermons* III/6, *op. cit.*, p. 44.

about with us, we endure infirmity, we look forward
to divinity. For God wishes not only to vivify, but
also to deify us. When would human infirmity ever
have dared to hope for this, unless divine truth had
promised it? Still, it was not enough for our God to
promise us divinity in himself, unless he also took
on our infirmity, as though to say, "Do you want to
know how much I love you, how certain you ought
to be that I am going to give you my divine reality?
I took to myself your mortal reality." We mustn't find
it incredible, brothers and sisters, that human beings
become gods, that is, that those who were human
beings become gods.[106]

How Augustinian is the opening to this beautifully crafted
sermon: our hearts are restless and they yearn for the security of divinity and the glories of godliness. That is what
causes consternation, that is what rouses us to follow our
dreams and desires—we are looking for the Lord but do
not always realize the goal of our journeys. So the Lord
comes to us, humbly promising us our sought-for divinity
by lowering himself to take on our broken humanity.

Although the term "deification" is not used in the Western Fathers as often as the equivalent "*theosis*" is found in
the East, the Latin writers used more understandable and
even biblical terms to teach this same divinizing reality, but
terms and images which could be received more easily by

[106] *Sermon* 23B.1; trans. Edmund Hill, *Sermons* III/11, *op. cit.*, p. 37;
this volume contains the thirty lost homilies of St. Augustine discovered by François Dolbeau since 1990.

their listeners. So, for example, a theology of deification could be more readily understood by employing the biblical terms of justification or sanctification, and this is how Augustine can so easily explain:

> Moreover, he who justifies is the same as he who deifies, because by justifying us he made us sons and daughters of God: *he gave them power to become children of God* (Jn 1:12). If we have been made children of God, we have been made into gods; but we are such by the grace of him who adopts us, not because we are of the same nature as the one who begets. Our Lord and Savior Jesus Christ is the unique Son of God; he is God, one God with the Father. . . . Others, who become gods, become so by his grace. They are not born of God's very being in such a way that they are what he is; it is through a gracious gift that they come to him and become with Christ his coheirs.[107]

We should conclude by appreciating how the bishop of Hippo translates such deification into liturgical language, for he knows that it is in the context of the daily Mass and in the sacraments of Christ's Church that the divine life is most securely and surely transmitted. Take, for example, a homily he gave to the newly baptized on the Easter Vigil of 404. He exhorts them to receive the grace of their baptism as their own becoming Eucharist, extensions and instantiations of the Body of Christ.

---

[107]   *Expositions on the Psalms* 49.2; trans. Maria Boulding III/16, p. 381.

So if it's you that are the Body of Christ and its
members, it's the mystery meaning you that has been
placed on the Lord's table; what you receive is the
mystery that means you. It is to what you are that
you reply *Amen*, and by so replying you express your
assent. What you hear, you see, is *The Body of Christ*,
and you answer, *Amen*. So, be a member of the body of
Christ, in order to make that *Amen* true.... Remember that bread is not made from one grain, but from
many. When you were being exorcised, it's as though
you were being ground. When you were baptized it's
as though you were mixed into dough. When you
received the fire of the Holy Spirit, it's as though you
were baked. Be what you can see, and receive what
you are.[108]

The Eucharistic Body on the altar is meant to be consumed
and so appropriated by the baptized elect. As that Host is
unified out of many and consecrated into a divine Person, so
too are the baptized meant to become Eucharist and thus be
the presence of Christ in their own families and communities. As such, Augustine's theology is not only theologically
deep, but also pastorally important, as he is never content
leaving doctrine in a book or piety in a devotion. Augustine
spent his life bringing the truths of the Catholic faith into
the personal and practical lives of those to whom he was
sent to minister, stressing their responsibility in becoming
Christ for the world. The baptized are the Body of Christ
in the world: as the Lord is present in the Eucharist, he is

---

[108]   Sermon 272; trans. Hill, *Sermons* III/7, *op. cit.*, pp. 297–98.

also present in his faithful people who pray only in order to become the arms and eyes, hands and hearts in the world of that Host reserved in the sanctuary.

The Council of Ephesus and Mary as the Mother of God

In many ways, these three Latin Fathers helped pave the way for an ecumenical council they neither envisioned nor ever attended (although Augustine had been invited, dying in 430 before the council was held). The main issue which this council had to address arose around 430 when St. Cyril, patriarch of Alexandria, accused Nestorius, the archbishop of Constantinople, of serious heresy. If the question of how the three divine Persons were related was the "hot button" issue of the fourth century, the question of how Jesus Christ's two natures were related was the most highly charged question of the fifth.

This clash between Cyril and Nestorius was the first serious sign that magisterial clarification regarding how one man can be both fully God and fully human was needed. The first rumblings of heresy came through the preaching of the very influential Bishop Nestorius of Constantinople who denied the unity of natures in Christ. Nestorius instead proposed a "two-subject Christology" wherein the divine Logos was simply conjoined to the human subject, the man of Jesus. As such, there was a sort of reservation regarding how the Word became flesh. Instead of a radical enfleshment, Nestorius preferred to talk about the unity of the divine and human natures in Christ as one of "likeness" or "appearance." Hence, Nestorius explained, "It is the temple that is capable of suffering, not the life-giving God of him who suffered."[109] By keeping the humanity and the divinity of Christ separate, Nestorius implies that the Savior was actually two subjects or two actors: one God and the other human, one the eternal Word and the other the Christ of salvation.

This way of understanding the Incarnation could have remained theologically abstract, but it had a direct impact on how the daily average Christian was living and worshipping. Namely, Nestorius's understanding of Christ kept him from calling Mary the "Mother of God," which Christians had been doing for centuries. Patriarch Nestorius rejected the term *Theotokos*, which means "God bearing," an ancient title attributed to Mary meaning "Mother of God." He instead preferred to invoke Mary as only the Christ-bearer, "*Christokos*," or even "*Theodokos*," meaning "God-receiving," but certainly not "God bearing."[110] Such an extreme separation of natures had two adverse results, the first doctrinal and the second more practical.

Nestorius, however, attempted to excuse or justify this thinking by claiming that while he may "hold the natures apart," he "unites the worship."[111] But how does divinity come into real and efficacious contact with humanity if the Lord Jesus is not one single agent? Also, if his divine and human natures never really act in unison or in harmony, how does his divinity heal our humanity? Even more seriously,

---

[109]   Cyril of Alexandria, *Against Nestorius*, trans. Norman Russell (London: Routledge, 2000), p. 160.

[110]   Nestorius, *Sermon 2*; quoted in J. N. D. Kelly, *Early Christian Doctrines*, rev. ed. (San Francisco: Harper, 1978), p. 316.

[111]   Nestorius, *Sermon 1*; quoted in J. N. D. Kelly, *op. cit.*, p. 312.

Nestorius's logic forced him to claim that as "regards the passion, God incarnate did not die, but God raised up him in whom God became incarnate."[112] That is, it was only the human Christ who suffered and died for us, not the Word himself; it was only the human Jesus who hungered in the desert and who wondered about the Father's day and hour. But if the incarnate Son of God did not, in the womb of his blessed mother, assume to himself, in a real and actual way, the entirety of the human condition, one wonders how the human condition has itself been healed. This was the doctrinal problem Nestorius forced the Church to clarify.

On a more practical level, Nestorius's understanding of Jesus rendered Mary of Bethlehem the mother of a human named Jesus but not the Mother of God. This is where the faithful voiced their disagreement, as devotion to the *Theotokos*, the *Mater Dei*, had been strong and only growing for centuries. The faithful were not to be deprived of their love of a woman who herself allowed the Son of God to enter his good creation. While admittedly being the "Mother of God" is quite a claim for any creature, it follows from the Christology hammered out during these years (as any Catholic doctrine is always really an outcome of the Church's thinking on the person of Christ).

In the year 430, Cyril of Alexandria (d. 444) arose and challenged Nestorius publicly, explaining to him that the One whom Mary conceived and gave birth to was truly the unique Word of God, God from God. "That is, taking flesh of the holy Virgin and making it his own from the womb,

---

[112]   Nestorius, *Sermon* I; quoted in Kelly, *op. cit.*, p. 316.

he underwent a birth like ours, and came forth a man from a woman, not throwing off what he was, but even though he became [man] by the assumption of flesh and blood, yet still remaining what he was, that is, God indeed in nature and truth."[113] In assuming the human condition immaculately and fully from Mary, God takes to himself what we are while never losing what he always is.

Cyril of Alexandria spent most of his later years responding to the Nestorian tendency to separate the Savior into two persons, one human and one divine. For instance, in his *Against Nestorius*, written in 430, St. Cyril challenged Nestorius and his followers by asking, "By faith in whom, then, are we justified? Is it not in him who suffered death according to the flesh for our sake? . . . If we had believed in a man like one of us rather than in God, this would have been dubbed anthropolatry [which means worship of a man]. . . . But if we believe that he who 'suffered in the flesh' (1 Pet. 4:1) is God, and that it is he who became our high priest, we have not erred in any way."[114] For Cyril, Nestorius's Christology was problematic because without the union of the divine and human natures in the person of Christ, the man Jesus is a mere "slave" who is "crowned with the glory that is proper to God," but who himself is only a mere substitute and representative rather than truly God.[115] Therefore, if we do in fact worship Jesus as Nesto-

---

[113]   Cyril of Alexandria, *ep*. 17.11, also known as the "Third Letter to Nestorius"; trans. Hardy, *Christology of the Later Fathers, op. cit,*. p. 353.
[114]   Cyril of Alexandria, *Against Nestorius*, trans. Norman Russell (London: Routledge, 2000), p. 166.
[115]   Cyril of Alexandria, *Unity of Christ* (a work lacking traditional section or chapter numbers), trans. John McGuckin (Crestwood, NY: St.

rius says he does, and if Jesus really is just a human—as Cyril cleverly challenges—Nestorius and his followers are nothing other than idolaters, anthropolaters, whose human Jesus cannot univocally and truly be the Christ of God as well. Furthermore, if that is true, Mary is not the Mother of God truly, but only the mother of Jesus's human nature.

While the term "anathema" (the Greek term for "detestable" or "accursed") sounds strong to our ears today, it is important to remember that fraternal correction is an important aspect of true charity. When your brother or sister goes astray, it is important to bring them back. That is why Cyril set a most serious tenor leading up to the Council of Ephesus by warning Nestorius to retract his heretical statements by laying out what the Church would come to teach about Christ and his blessed mother in his *Third Letter to Nestorius*, which contains his *twelve anathemas*. Cyril's twelve anathemas are very strongly put, and their impact would be realized through the deposition of Nestorius from ecclesial office and his eventual exile. In some ways, all twelve could be read as inflections of the first: "If anyone does not confess that Emmanuel is God in truth, and therefore the *Holy Virgin Theotokos*—for she bore in the flesh the Word of God became flesh—let him be anathema."[116] Thereafter, Cyril stresses how the union between Jesus's perfect divinity and perfect humanity is not merely moral or accidental but hypostatic, personal, and eternal (nos. 2 and 3). Furthermore, this union cannot be

---

Vladimir's Press, 1995), p. 76.
[116] "The Third Letter of Cyril to Nestorius," 1st Anathema; trans. Hardy, *Christology of the Later Fathers, op. cit,*. p. 353.

divided, and therefore, the humanity of Christ is one with his divinity and therefore salvific; Jesus is therefore not just a "God-bearer" (*Theophorus*), but truly God and worthy of all adoration and obedience (nos. 4–10).

The eleventh anathema follows discussion of Christ as our High Priest, not by the ordination of the Holy Spirit, but through his very nature. Cyril thereby reminds us that the flesh of Jesus Christ is truly one with his divinity and that it is in that very flesh he offered himself, as our priest and the lamb of sacrifice, both on Calvary and still today at every Mass: "If anyone does not confess that the flesh of the Lord is life-giving, and the own [flesh] of the Word of God the Father, but as of another besides him, associated with him in dignity, or having received merely a divine indwelling—and not rather life-giving, as we have said, because it became the own [flesh] of the Word who is able to give life to all things, let him be anathema."[117] Again, the point he is emphasizing is this: this is the very flesh Bishop Cyril knew he offered the faithful at every Mass. This is the very same flesh to which we have access still today.

When these warnings were delivered to Nestorius, he sought Emperor Theodosius II's confirmation and asked for a fair hearing in return; Cyril, on the other hand, asked Pope Celestine I to call upon Nestorius to recant. It was thus decided that the Church would hold her third ecumenical council in the city where, either coincidentally or providentially, the Greek world had honored Artemis, a goddess associated with fertility, to declare Mary officially

---

[117]   11th Anathema; Hardy, *op. cit.*, p. 354.

as *Theotokos*, the Mother of God. In the summer months of 431, then, 250 bishops from all over the known Christian world gathered in Ephesus to work out a Christology that honored what the Sacred Scriptures told about Jesus, how the Christian people worshipped Jesus, and how the Christian people understood and approached their beloved Mother Mary.

The Council Fathers were fairly uniform in their deliberations, drawing from earlier tradition, especially from the Alexandrian inclination to keep the natures of Christ united, and not from the Antiochene tendency to stress the two nature's differences. As a result, Nestorius was condemned and removed from his episcopal see. The Church now officially declared that Jesus Christ is to be understood as one divine person in two inseparable natures, both fully God and fully human. As a result, Mary could be legitimately and piously invoked as the Mother of the Son of God now made flesh. In truth, if Jesus is God, Mary is rightly and truly the Mother of God.

As we shall see in the next chapter, although the council's decision should have brought closure to a fiery debate, it lingered on in the theological camps in and around Ephesus. The mystery of the Incarnation is easily violated when the unity of natures is overly-stressed, which collapses the divine and human nature into each other, or when one over-emphasizes the distinction between these two natures, thus dividing the Christ into two separate actors. To preserve the beauty of the Incarnation, then, bishops, theologians, preachers, and the people continued to debate and discuss, they continued to pray, but they also sought to secure the most influential and helpful political power possible.

Yet, if all the theological ramifications of the Incarnation were not satisfactorily discerned or determined at Ephesus, the truth that was declared was certainly emphasized liturgically. Fortunately, we possess the homilies delivered by the main celebrant of the Masses held during the time of Ephesus, and when we listen to Proclus (d. 446), bishop of Constantinople, we hear a theology that is so beautifully sensitive to the contours of Scripture and the intertwining lives depicted there of Mary, her Son, and all their spiritual family:

> She who called us here today is the Holy Mary; the untarnished vessel of virginity; the spiritual paradise of the Second Adam; the workshop for the union of natures; the market-place of the contract of salvation, the bridal chamber in which the Word took the flesh in marriage, the living bush of human nature, which the fire of a divine birth-pang did not consume; the veritable swift cloud who carried in her body the one who rides upon the cherubim; the purest fleece drenched with the rain which came down from heaven, whereby the shepherd clothed himself with the sheep. . . . The loom-worker was the Holy Spirit; the woolworker the overshadowing power from on high.[118]

---

[118] Proclus of Constantinople, *Homily 1.1*; trans. Nicholas Constas, *Proclus of Constantinople and the Cult of the Virgin in Late Antiquity— Homilies 1-5* (Leiden: Brill, 2003), p. 137.

As important as this history of the early councils is, it is even more important to realize that Catholic truths are never antiquated museum pieces but living and transformative invitations. That is why even today we can see the theology that was hammered out in ancient Ephesus alive in current teaching, as the *Catechism* clearly states: "Called in the Gospels 'the mother of Jesus,' Mary is acclaimed by Elizabeth, at the prompting of the Spirit and even before the birth of her son, as 'the mother of my Lord.' In fact, the One whom she conceived as man by the Holy Spirit, who truly became her Son according to the flesh, was none other than the Father's eternal Son, the second Person of the Holy Trinity. Hence the Church confesses that Mary is truly 'Mother of God' (*Theotokos*)."[119]

Mary protects both the humanity and the divinity of Jesus. She is, of course, not divine, but she is as close to divinity as any creature can get. She is the daughter of the Father, the mother of the Son, and the spouse of the Holy Spirit. Ephesus made it clear that it is not a question of Jesus or Mary but rather Jesus and Mary. The mission of Mary was to conceive Jesus in her heart by faith and then conceive him in her womb by the Holy Spirit, and thus bring him to others, as she first began to do at the Annunciation and Visitation.[120]

---

[119]   CCC §495.

[120]   For a whimsical look at the life of Mary, see my *101 Surprising Facts about Mary* (TAN Books, 2020).

Conclusion

Whereas the fourth-century Church still had to contend with anti-Catholic persecutions and its aftereffects, it also had to refute numerous heresies, especially Christologies which rendered the Son of God less than fully divine. The Church in the fifth century, on the other hand, was free to excel and concentrate on more subtle theological questions. The Church could now define more aspects of culture. Bishops were able to exert more influence, and the faithful were able to make their voices known more widely. Those who wrote and preached in order to defend and promote the Faith were able to draw from a longer line of tradition and thus proceed in a more systematic and sophisticated way.

After the age of the Apostolic Fathers, who addressed basic Church discipline and proper rites of worship, came that of the Apologists who appealed to both Greek wisdom and Jewish prophecy to demonstrate that Christianity was the fulfilment of a divine plan rather than a danger to society. It was Christianity that showed what God was really doing through Socrates and Moses. After the legalization of Christianity in 313, a new era dawned, and the Church produced the great Church Fathers—Athanasius, Basil, Gregory Nazianzen, and John Chrysostom in the East, and Ambrose, Jerome, Augustine, and Pope Gregory the Great in the West. This chapter concentrated on the first three of these four Latin Fathers (with Gregory dying in 604 and thus falling outside our five-hundred-year scope), showing how the Body of Christ was first formed through the faith of Mother Mary and then, through her intercession, continues to be formed mystically in the Church's sons and daughters.

From St. Augustine, we have the wonderful concept of "the whole Christ"—a realistic understanding that Jesus Christ is not just a single man now ascended into heaven. The "whole Christ" is Jesus as well as all those whom Jesus loves, forming one mystical person just as love forms many into one family. For a mother and a father feel incomplete without their children, and if that is true for us who are sinful and at times rejoice wrongly in our autonomy, how much more so is it true for the perfectly loving God-man who came only to be united with those who long to be one with him. This unfolding of Christ's life into the lives of Christians is a constant throughout Church teaching, and it received an important grounding in the works of the Churchmen treated here, even if throughout the ages we see this truth expressed in various ways.

Who Do You Say that I Am?

PETER SPEAKS THROUGH LEO AT THE COUNCIL OF CHALCEDON (451)

"Now it happened that as he was praying alone the disciples were with him; and he asked them, 'Who do the people say that I am?' And they answered, John the Baptist; but others say, Elijah; and others, that one of the old prophets has risen.' And he said to them, 'But who do you say that I am?' And Peter answered, 'The Christ of God'" (Lk 9:18–20).

So FAR, WE have seen how the first major question Christ's Church had to answer was the relationship between this man Jesus and the one true God. Was Jesus a man endowed with divine powers or truly God who had become truly human? As the Church grew, she began to ask more subtle and complex questions about her Lord and Lover. Although the internal relationships of the Godhead were officially pronounced—that both the Son (Nicaea in 325) and the Spirit (I Constantinople in 381) are eternally consubstantial with and equally divine as God the Father—questions remained regarding the most faithful ways to envision and speak of the Savior's relationship with his mother (Ephesus

in 431) and how he could be truly both God and human
(Chalcedon in 451).

"Who do you say that I am?" might therefore be the
most important question any creature could ever be asked.
This is the one question which alone determines an eternal destiny, and the Church's answering of this question is
where this final chapter begins and where this slim volume
ends. At the Council of Chalcedon in 451, the finer intri-
cacies of who this Jesus Christ is were worked out under
the guidance and through the teachings of Pope Leo, in
line with the trusted voices of this great Tradition, what
G. K. Chesterton calls "the democracy of the dead." Drawing from many of the figures we have already met, the
Council of Chalcedon laid down the ways in which we
are able to think and speak correctly about the incarnate
Son of God. How did the man Jesus Christ access divine
knowledge? Did he really not know "the day or the hour" of
the *Parousia*, as the inerrant Scriptures attest (Mk 13:32)?
Did God really hunger in the desert and did he really die
on the cross, or was this just the human nature of Jesus
which showed such finitude and mortality? If he really is
both God and man, how are these two natures related, how
do they interact? Are they separable or do his humanity and
divinity somehow act independently from one another?

This chapter starts by tracing the various ways this
human Messiah was conceived of over the centuries leading up to the Council of Chalcedon. As we trace this history of mortals peering into the ultimate mystery of God's
becoming human, we shall encounter again some figures
met earlier and some new ones as well. After this history,

we shall move to the fallout after the Council of Ephesus and the subsequent Formula of Union of 433.

This approach will enable us to see how important areas of the Christian world tended to think of and describe Christ in distinct ways, and the ways in which bishops labored to keep these two opposing tendencies together. Then we will consider the proceedings and significance of the fourth ecumenical council. Finally, we will conclude with a section offering a spirituality of ecclesiology as a capstone to our examination of the relationship between history and theology, this tracing of how and why Christ founded a Church in order to ensure his life and love could be acknowledged, approached, and assimilated.

A Lingering Debate and the Beginnings of Monophysitism

Was the Arianism we examined back in chapter 3 a Trinitarian or a Christological problem? Could it have been both? If the Son of God is not fully and consubstantially divine with the Father, how could that incarnate Son save us? Would he not instead simply have to point the way to the One who could? The tensions which the heresy of Arius uncovered and exacerbated would continue in different ways and in various magnitudes for centuries: How do Christians keep unity and otherness in proper relationship? That is, how can monotheists profess faith in a Trinity of divine Persons, and how can one of those divine Persons come to live perfectly and harmoniously in two natures? Was the Nestorianism we read about in the previous chapter a Marian or Christological problem? Could it have been both? If the Babe of

Bethlehem really is God incarnate, how do we explain the maternal role of one who came chronologically well after this One who was born? How can God have a mother, and what does this say about the role of a creature in giving life to Life himself? As the fourth century gave way to the fifth century, these questions remained and two camps emerged, diametrically opposed in how they spoke about the incarnate Lord and what about him they felt necessary to stress.

Throughout the latter fourth and through the fifth century, a growing rift emerged between the ways these two groups thought about the person of Jesus Christ. In Alexandria were those who invoked the great names of the famous catechetical school there—Clement of Alexandria, Origen, and of course Athanasius and Cyril—thinkers who all stressed Christ's unity and the deifying effect his incarnation has on his Church. The other way of conceiving of the Incarnation was associated with those in Antioch who tended to follow the exegesis of Lucian of Antioch (martyred in 312) and his tendency to distinguish the separate natures of Christ. It was the human historicity of the Messiah that really mattered, and we should be careful not to confuse Christ's eternal divinity with the humanity he brought to himself in time.

While dividing any historical movement or development into two overly-facile categories is admittedly dangerous, this dichotomy helps us see obvious tendencies: whereas Alexandrians tended to unite, Antiochenes tended to divide. While both unity and distinction admittedly have their place in orthodox Christian theology, the fifth century forced thinkers to define and distinguish like never before.

Throughout the history of Christ's apostolic Church, major councils officially clarified some teaching while sometimes unleashing even more questions leading to ever more theological and political factions. We have seen how Arianism splintered and spread after Nicaea, and we now find ourselves in those decades after Ephesus when differing Christological approaches were increasingly promoted and opposed one another with vitriol and suspicion.

As we saw in the previous chapter, Nestorius's supposed suspicion of making too close a union between the eternal Word and the humanity of Jesus Christ affected not only Christological doctrine but, what was even more important to many, popular devotion. Can we say that Mary really gave birth to God? Did God really die for our sins on Calvary? These were the questions Cyril needed to answer and the answers he worked to provide so swiftly and strongly at Ephesus. But perhaps Cyril responded too brutally, excommunicating Nestorius, demanding a public signing of his anathemas. This put Cyril and the pope whom he had brought to his side in strong opposition to the emperor and the recently consecrated Bishop John I of Antioch (d. 441). Cyril's arrogance was obvious to all, and when his supporter Pope Celestine died in 432 (replaced by the holy but much more Western-looking Pope Sixtus III, a good friend of St. Augustine's, who helped construct much of Rome's ecclesial infrastructure seen today), a new chapter opened. Cyril suddenly felt he needed to explain the Alexandrian position in a manner more palatable to the Antiochenes who now seemed to have the political sway in their favor.

Cyril came to see that in order to ensure that the Christ would never again be denigrated to a lower divine status, the Antiochenes took a very anti-Arian position in stressing that in Jesus there was one divine hypostasis, clearly the Son of God, and another wherein he assumed the fullness of humanity, the Son of Mary. Important figures like Bishop Diodore of Tarsus (d. c. 390) and the influential biblical commentator Theodore of Mopsuestia (d. 428) united these two natures by such a strong union that the divinity and humanity never contradicted each other and yet acted in perfect unison in the person of Jesus Christ. This union was seen as one of voluntary harmony and moral perfection. This was the Antiochene inclination, to keep the two natures of Jesus separate. Interestingly, this tendency to separate is also how the Antiochenes tended to read Sacred Scripture. Unlike the Alexandrian penchant for allegory and deep symbolism, the Antiochenes approached the Old Testament literally and historically only, separating the events of Israel carefully from the Church's life, tending to downplay any allegorical or symbolic interpretations as arbitrary and therefore fanciful.

In the end, the moral union stressed by the Antiochenes was found insufficient in explaining the unity of the Word made flesh, and that is why Cyril of Alexandria stressed the "hypostatic," or wholly personal, union of Christ's divinity when assuming the fullness of humanity in the womb of his mother. Alexandrian thinkers had worked assiduously to stress the unity of natures in Christ, that it was the God-man who as the agent of our salvation. Those working from the Alexandrian school thus stressed the unified work of the one Word-made-flesh, while also tending to read the Scriptures in a positively allegorical way which saw the relationship of Jesus and the individual soul or the collective Church on almost every page of both the Old and the New Testaments. Instead of a link or union between natures, the Alexandrians tended instead to rely on Athanasius's tighter phraseology, the *Logos ensarkos*—the enfleshed Logos, desirous to unify divine spirit and human creatureliness (body and soul) as intimately as the soul is with the body.

What seemed to be a Christological impasse eventually gave way to a *Formulary of Reunion* in 433, basically protecting the Antiochene stressing of distinction while honoring the Alexandrian understanding of the essential importance of unity: "our Lord Jesus Christ, the unique Son of God, perfect God and perfect man, of a reasonable soul and body; begotten of the Father before [the] ages according to the Godhead, and consubstantial with us in his manhood, for a union of two natures took place; therefore we confess one Christ, one Son, one Lord."[121] It would be this phrase, "union of two natures," that seemed to confirm the Alexandrian stress on unity, while also putting to rest the Nestorian fear of only one nature after the union. This Formula of Union was temporarily acceptable to both Cyril and John of Antioch. But when Cyril eventually died in 444, partisan memories reemerged and the new leader of Antiochene theology, Theodoret of Cyr (d. c. 457), was strongly attacked by Cyril's replacement, Dioscorus (d. 454), the new patriarch of Alexandria.

---

[121] *Formulary of Union* as in Hardy, *Christology of Later Fathers, op. cit.*, p. 356.

In fact, Dioscorus was filled with nothing but antipathy for the Antiochene approach which wanted to keep the two natures of Christ distinct. He feared that separation so much that he sided with a highly influential monk who stressed the unity of Christ's two natures to such a degree that the Lord's humanity was subsumed into his divinity, as a drop of water is absorbed into a sea of wine. This monk was Eutyches (d. 456) who had been condemned by Dioscorus's rival, the new Bishop Flavian of Constantinople. To embarrass Flavian, Dioscorus curried the favor of Theodosius II (d. 450) and had the emperor declare another council which would rehabilitate Eutyches and show how his version of Monophysitism was in fact the most accurate way to understand the person of Jesus. If Nestorianism was the extreme approach to keeping the natures of Christ distinct in such a way that the humanity and divinity are joined only by moral harmony or agreement in acting in unison, Monophysitism must be seen as the extreme approach wherein the divinity overrides the humanity in such a way that the manhood of the Savior is led dragging behind but itself does not really act or in any way influence the divine Word's life on earth.

Theodosius II was certainly no theologian, but he was careful to do what he could to keep his Christian populace united. Like Constantine, he cared less about dogma and doctrinal accuracy than he did about civic harmony. A cagey politician, Theodosius II knew that he should somehow address this condemnation of the popular Eutyches, so he summoned a council at Ephesus yet again. In November, 448, Theodosius appointed Dioscorus of Alexandria to lead this reinvestigation. Not surprisingly, Eutyches's Christology was found to be wholly orthodox. He was therefore acquitted of all heresy and reinstated as the archimandrite of his monastery in Constantinople. Flavian and the more moderate bishops were all deposed and the Roman representatives were dismissed without any due hearing.

When Theodosius II died the following year, Pope Leo took this opportunity to write to the emperor's wonderfully Catholic sister who was elevated to empress upon the death of her brother. Pope Leo appealed to Empress Pulcheria's devotion to the ancient Roman Church as having magisterial primacy in all doctrinal matters, and famously indicated to her that what occurred at the sham council of Ephesus II could in no way be considered either truly conciliar or binding. In fact, it was instead a "Robber's Council" where truth had been stolen—or in the pope's memorable Latin phrase, this synod was not a gathering of sound judgment but of hired thieves: *non iudicium, sed latrocinium*. Later that year of 450, Pulcheria married Marcian and together helped Pope Leo make his Christology known more intelligently and as worthy of acceptance in the East, thus binding for all.

Pope Leo and the Council of Chalcedon

Leo's triumph was in sight when Emperor Marcian declared the recent proceedings of Ephesus II invalid and instead called around six hundred bishops to Chalcedon just across the Bosphorus—not far from the imperial palace in Constantinople—in order not to disrupt the emperor's daily tasks too much. On October 8 in 451, the bishops gathered at Chalcedon and began by affirming the teachings of Nicaea and Constantinople and then annulling the "Robber Council" held just two years prior, stating that it was illicitly convened and that no teaching from it could be regarded as authentic Catholic doctrine.

The Council of Chalcedon is foundationally important for any understanding of the Church. It is the fourth and final ecumenical council that all major Christian denominations adhere to as binding. It is the council which gave rise to non-Chalcedonian Orthodox Christian groups still numerous today, like the Coptic Christians, the Syriac Orthodox Church, the Armenian Church, the Malankara Orthodox Syrian Church (mainly in India), the Ethiopian Orthodox, and other smaller communities. The Council of Chalcedon is celebrated for providing the Church with her most definitive Trinitarian and Christological formulas, but it also is important for the very controversial move of sanctioning the grand title of patriarch for the rightful bishops of major apostolic sees (e.g., Jerusalem and Antioch) and even going further to assign the honor due to the bishop of Rome to the patriarch of "the New Rome," Constantinople. Of course, Leo and all popes thereafter have rejected that equation. Thus, we can see in the Council of Chalcedon the seedcorn for the Great Schism between East and West much later in 1054.

Testimonial to the Church's unbroken continuity, many of these battles at Chalcedon are succinctly explained in the *Catechism of the Catholic Church*. Under the *Catechism's* section on the Incarnation, "True God and True Man," the Church teaches:

> The Monophysites affirmed that the human nature had ceased to exist as such in Christ when the divine person of God's Son assumed it. Faced with this heresy, the fourth ecumenical council, at Chalcedon in 451, confessed:
>
> "Following the holy Fathers, we unanimously teach and confess one and the same Son, our Lord Jesus Christ: the same perfect in divinity and perfect in humanity, the same truly God and truly man, composed of rational soul and body; consubstantial with the Father as to his divinity and consubstantial with us as to his humanity; 'like us in all things but sin'. He was begotten from the Father before all ages as to his divinity and in these last days, for us and for our salvation, was born as to his humanity of the virgin Mary, the Mother of God.
>
> "We confess that one and the same Christ, Lord, and only-begotten Son, is to be acknowledged in two natures without confusion, change, division or separation. The distinction between the natures was never abolished by their union, but rather the character proper to each of the two natures was preserved as they came together in one person (*prosopon*) and one hypostasis."[122]

---

[122] CCC §467.

The *Catechism* lifts this section of the conciliar proceedings because it contains not only the recognition that confessing Christ as one divine person in two natures is a constant from the Church's treasury of Faith ("Following the holy Fathers..."), it also provides contemporary philosophical language with which to guide any generation's understanding of the Incarnation.

The four Chalcedonian adverbs found here seek to ensure that Jesus Christ is understood to be one divine Person who assumed the fullness of humanity to himself in such a way that his humanity and his divinity are wholly unified unconfusedly, unchangeably, indivisibly, and inseparably. Notice the intellectual humility in professing these adverbs as canonical: they do not insist on how we must describe the Incarnation, but they instead set limits on what we cannot say has occurred in the mystery of God's becoming human. We cannot speak in a way which implies that the two natures may have become either mingled or have been altered in some way; nor can we say that any one of these two natures functions apart from the other.

In other words, the human and divine natures are without confusion, meaning that the two natures of Christ never confound or disrupt the other, nor do they combine to form some third hybrid being, but Christ is always and everywhere both fully human as well as fully divine. Second, these natures are without change, meaning that now in perfect unity, they are not altered into something they were not before: Christ's perfect human nature is always human and his divine nature remains ever divine. The Second Person of the Trinity does not lessen his divinity in becoming human, nor is his sinless humanity made more than what it was in being assumed to divinity. Thirdly, these natures are without division. Against Nestorius, there was never—nor could there ever be—a humanity of Jesus Christ divided against or dwelling independently from his divinity. The humanity of Christ began and now eternally dwells as one with his divinity from the moment of Mary's yes, and at no time before. Henceforth, it was the Word made flesh as one who is both wholly God and wholly man and not just some part of one interacting with a part of the other nature. Finally, the term "inseparable" solidifies this understanding that one nature never acts independently from the other. It is not as if Christ puts his divinity away in order to hunger or to die, nor does he put his humanity aside in order to work miracles.

These four adverbs, insisting on the total unity of and full cooperation between our Savior's eternal divinity and assumed humanity, led theologians at Chalcedon to declare what came to be called the *communicatio idiomatum*—the communication of idioms. This phrase leads us to a consideration of a most beautiful aspect of the way in which Christ acts. To communicate is to predicate an attribute to a particular thing and an idiom is a self-contained reality. Consequently, the communication of idioms means that whatever one predicates of one nature of Christ, one can say of the other nature as well. Think of what this means: it was not just the humanity of Christ which died on Calvary, it was his divinity too, and so one can legitimately and boldly proclaim God's love because God died on the cross. Conversely, it is not just the divinity of Christ which rose on Easter morning, it was his humanity too, and so one can legitimately and boldly proclaim humanity's deification because humanity defeated death in that now empty tomb.

Chalcedon thus insisted that whatever we "communicate" of one "idiom" or nature, we must say of the other nature as well. So, in Christ, we can literally say that this man is God and that God is this man. We can now announce that in Christ, God himself is born, or that God himself is literally crucified on a cross. What the communication of idioms rightly disallows is our tendency to ascribe seemingly human functions simply to Christ's human nature while attributing the mighty and majestic acts only to his divinity: in Christ, God thirsts and man forgives sins. Behind this way of speaking is the insistence that it is a person who is conceived, who is born, who acts, and who dies and rises, not a nature. Of course such language goes only for the Second Person of the Trinity who has become flesh out of love for humankind; one cannot, of course, ascribe these human properties to the Father or to the Holy Spirit but only to the God-man Jesus Christ. That is, even though one can say that God dies on Good Friday, one cannot say that it is the Father or it is the Holy Spirit who perishes for the sins of fallen humanity. One cannot say that the Father is born in Bethlehem or the Spirit is tempted in the desert, but one can surely say that God is born on Christmas and that God himself assumes our struggles against sin.

Chalcedon thus saw itself as continuing and clarifying the Good News of the Beloved Son's becoming human. Those bishops who drafted the proceedings of Chalcedon saw in their words a Christian story which is organic, assimilative, and one which approaches rightly all that Christ revealed consistently through all ages. In their combatting any remnant of Nestorianism and in their rejection of the newer Monophysitism, Chalcedon stayed on the right path in navigating between these two extremes, the Council Fathers quoted Scripture, Athanasius, Cyril, and of course the latest leader of Christological orthodoxy, Leo of Rome.

In the second session of Chalcedon, a large section of a letter which Leo wrote to Flavian to help him against Dioscorus and Eutyches was read. This selection, cut from epistle 28 of Pope Leo to Bishop Flavian, is today known as *The Tome*, as "tome" comes from the Greek word to cut or break off (the a-tom, for example, used to be thought of as the smallest indivisible particle of reality). Not much is known of Leo's life before being made pope in 440. Like most of the Roman clergy at this time, he was born to already Catholic parents, received a very good classical education, and offered himself to the Diocese of Rome. Quickly recognized for his wisdom and wit, Leo was utilized for diplomatic missions around the empire. Leo was in Gaul (now modern France) when he received the word that the Roman clergy had elected him the next pope in the autumn of 440.

One hundred sermons and approximately 150 letters have come down to us from Leo's pontificate. In these, we see a very busy administrator whose theological output consists in helping others understand and address particular situations, theological as well as political. We meet a wise and loving pastor who insists on the deification of Christ's mystical body. To achieve that union of Christ and Christian, the first and foundational insistence must be on unity, a theme Leo stresses often but perhaps most intentionally when writing to the Empress Pulcheria. Responding to one of her letters, the pope replies, "In [your letter] you clearly show how much you love the Catholic faith and how much you despise the errors of heretics." Heresy is most pernicious for one so insistent on ecclesial harmony as Leo, and as one who understands the context of the mid-fifth century, he continues, "Heresy denies that the eternal Son of the eternal Father took from the womb of the blessed Virgin Mary the real flesh of our nature, and it attacks with condemnation those who could not be led away from the evangelical and apostolic faith by any error."[123]

All of this acknowledged, orthodox doctrine remains a mental category only if it is not appropriated by the heart. That is why it is not enough simply to believe and preach the Incarnation rightly; God's sacred enfleshment must also be received and incorporated into who one longs to become. Our great bishop can therefore preach, and often does, on the Most Holy Eucharist, that "celestial food" which is not only evidence of God's becoming flesh but our invitation to become God: "This partaking in the body and blood of Christ means nothing else than that we should pass over into what we have taken in."[124] In his writings, Pope Leo stressed such a convergence, that Christ passes into us in

---

[123] Leo the Great, *Epistle* 60; trans. Edmund Hunt, C.S.C. (New York: Fathers of the Church Inc., 1957), p. 132.
[124] Leo the Great, *Sermon* 64.7; trans. Jane Freeland, C.S.J.B. (Washington, DC: Catholic University of America, 1996), p. 277.

order that we might pass over into him and thus experience the newness of life promised in the Spirit, attainable only through Christ's Church.

This newness can never be taken for granted. Leo is the consummate curator of souls, knowing on a profound level the fragility of the earthen vessel in whicheach of us holds our eternal treasure. On Christmas morning in Rome in 440, then, he shall preach to his congregation and remind them ever so gently that they can never forget to preserve carefully the new life within them through ecclesial devotion and fraternal charity, concluding his sermon with this exhortation:

> Realize, O Christian, your dignity. Once made a "partaker in the divine nature" (2 Pet 1:4), do not return to your former baseness unworthy of that dignity. Remember whose head it is and whose body of which you constitute a member. Recall how you have been wrested "from the power of darkness and brought into the light and the kingdom" of God (Col 1:13). Through the Sacrament of Baptism you were made a "temple of the Holy Spirit" (1 Cor 6:19). Do not drive away such a dweller by your wicked actions and subject yourself again to servitude under the devil, because your price is the very blood of Christ. Because he will judge you in truth who has redeemed you in mercy, Christ our Lord. Amen.[125]

---

[125]   Leo the Great, *Sermon* 21.3; trans. Freeland, *op. cit.*, p. 79.

Leo's Christology is an obvious mirror of his soteriology: God assumes humanity to his own divine nature because he longs to bring human persons into the life of his own divine perfection. The paradox Leo points out in this great exchange is that at one point we were both in need to make this exchange a reality. Or put this way, as God in himself cannot die, we humans in and of ourselves cannot truly live. Therefore, in order that true life might be restored to those made in his image and likeness, in order that we might attain a life not naturally our own, God himself first took on a nature not his own—namely, our sinful flesh.

Pope Leo thus realized that divinity pure and simple could never suffer (in fact, divinity alone can never become anything). Yet, once united with the human nature offered to God by Mary, now the eternally Begotten Son can be born in time, now Life himself can be crucified and the Almighty can be contained in a tomb. This is an aspect of the Good News Leo enjoys highlighting for his flock: God saves us not from the outside but from within the very condition you and I inherited as children of Eve, defeats death as we are, fights for us as one of us, where we live so to speak and not from a distant heaven. God could have saved us the way he spoke to the Old Testament holy men and women, Leo surmises, but that would not have been as beautiful, lacking an intimacy that only a face-to-face encounter can achieve. As he wrote to the empress Pulcheria on June 13, 449:

> Wisdom building herself a house within Mary's undefiled body, the Word became flesh; and the form

of God and the form of a slave coming together into one person, the Creator of times was born in time; and he himself through whom all things were made, was brought forth in the midst of all things. For if the New Man had not been made in the likeness of sinful flesh, and taken on him our old nature, and being consubstantial with the Father, had deigned to be consubstantial with his mother also, and being alone free from sin, had united our nature to him [if he had not done these things] the whole human race would be held in bondage beneath the Devil's yoke, and we should not be able to make use of the Conqueror's victory, if it had been won outside our nature.[126]

The mysteries of Christ's life receive their full potential only when we take them up and make them our own. We must experience what Christ did if we are ever going to receive the healed humanity the enfleshed Word offers us.

During the Good Friday liturgy in 453, Leo preached that since our fallen human state must be "healed of its ancient wounds and purified from its off-scouring of sin, the Only-Begotten of God became also the son of a human being." The Christ did this, Leo the theologian reminds us, so that "he would not lack either the whole reality of human nature or the fullness of divinity."[127] Pope Leo then continues, explicating this union in terms not only of God's taking on our life but also how we too must take on his—not

---

[126] Leo the Great, *Epistle* 31.2 to the Empress Pulcheria (June 13, 449); trans. Charles Lett Feltoe, *Nicene and Post-Nicene Fathers*, op. cit., vol. 12, p. 45.

[127] Leo the Great, *Sermon* 66.4; trans. Freeland, *op.cit.*, p. 289.

just in an abstract way but literally by making the events of Jesus's life ours as well:

> Consequently, just as it was our nature (joined into one with the divinity) that the virginity of his Mother brought forth, so it was ours also that the Jewish wickedness crucified. What lay lifeless was ours, and what rose on the third day was ours, as well as what ascended above the heights of heaven to the right hand of the Father's majesty. If we walk in the way of his commandments and if we are not ashamed to confess that which brings our salvation in the humility of the body, we too will be brought into the company of his glory.[128]

In becoming a man, Leo emphasizes, Christ offers us a share of his own divine life. Because Christ has thus "transformed all the members of his body into himself," we too cry out on the cross, we too do battle with the enemy of our human nature, but it is also we who shall reign glorious as the eternal children of God in heaven.

The way Leo approached the Incarnation made him the perfect pope under whom the Church's major Christological council should be held. It is clear from his preaching about the Trinity, Leo unquestionably incorporated the language of Nicaea by stressing how the Son is consubstantial with the Father and that the Trinity is one nature in three persons. It is also clear that Leo prepares the way for the final word on the Incarnation as he easily weaves

---

[128] Ibid., pp. 289–90.

the theology of Christ's being one divine Person with two natures easily into his pastoral concerns. By becoming fully human and uniting our own lives into his own, Jesus Christ offers us a share in his filiality before the Father, as well as in his suffering and subsequent resurrection.

Whereas the Nestorians wanted to posit one nature per one person, thus viewing Christ as one divine person and one human person and the Monophysites desired an even more simplistic "one nature" theory of Christ's divinity consuming his humanity, Pope Leo was uniquely poised to direct the proceedings of Chalcedon to a profound and true expression of the union of Christ's humanity and divinity, giving divinity the ability to communicate itself to humans and elevating humanity so it now can be perfectly one with God.

Having a unique sense of the empire gleaned from his years as a diplomat, one of the first things Leo did was to secure the Church's jurisdiction over all the Western sees, receiving from Emperor Valentinian III a rescript recognizing unassailable papal power over the Church, finally wresting her away from the emperor's desire to manage and control Church affairs not only in Italy but in Spain, Gaul, and Roman Africa as well. Leo's influence in the East was not as easily recognizable until the Monophysite controversy became the means by which his help and orthodox doctrine would be known. In his *Tome*, Leo briefly and brilliantly insists on the two nature Christology of Flavian and shows how these two natures interact.

Leo begins with something we should all keep in mind, that when facing the fundamental mysteries of Christianity,

one can turn either to the authority of the Gospels or to
oneself, either to the Church or to the self, and in so doing,
one becomes either a disciple of the truth or a teacher of
error. He has Eutyches firmly in his crosshairs as he argues
that the savior of the human race must be simultaneously a
God who can save as well as a human who can communicate his life to all who come to him, and in this assumption
of humanity into divinity, a new way of life is thus available
to us:

> Accordingly, while the distinctness of both natures
> and substances was preserved, and both met in one
> Person, lowliness was assumed by majesty, weakness
> by power, mortality by eternity; and, in order to pay
> the debt of our condition, the inviolable nature was
> united to the passible, so that as the appropriate rem-
> edy for our ills, one and the same "Mediator between
> God and man, the Man Christ Jesus," might from
> one element be capable of dying and also from the
> other be incapable. Therefore in the entire and perfect
> nature of very man was born very God, whole in what
> was his, whole in what was ours.[129]

This union of humanity and divinity in Jesus Christ is our
unity as well: while keeping each nature distinct and unal-
tered, Christ assumes all that we are to himself in order to
remedy what makes the human condition so arduous and
moribund. Our lowliness, our weakness, our ills, and even
our mortality have all been alleviated, not through forensic

---

[129]　Leo the Great, *Tome* §3; trans. Hardy, *op. cit.*, p. 363.

power from above but from intimate love from within. God takes to himself all that we fear and renders our fallen state something beautiful through love.

This is why, Leo continues, the Son of God left his heavenly homeland and assumed the role of the New Adam in whom all of Eden's exiles can find a new home, a new identity, a new eternity:

> Accordingly, the Son of God, descending from his seat in heaven, and not departing from the glory of the Father, enters this lower world, born after a new order, by a new mode of birth. After a new order; because he who in his own sphere is invisible, became visible in ours; he who could not be enclosed in space, willed to be enclosed; continuing to be before times, he began to exist in time; the Lord of the universe allowed his infinite majesty to be overshadowed, and took upon him the form of a servant; the impassible God did not disdain to be passible Man and the immortal One to be subjected to the laws of death.[130]

Acting in perfect unison, divinity is not changed in its descent into humanity and humanity is not consumed by its union with divinity: each acts in perfect communion with the other nature, yet it is the Word who performs every act inseparably as both God and man.

With Leo's Christology clearly holding sway in the deliberations, each bishop present was told to offer a written statement affirming the main tenets of Nicaea, I

---

[130]   Leo the Great, *Tome* §4; trans. Hardy, *op. cit.*, p. 364.

Constantinople, and the Christology of Athanasius, Cyril of Alexandria, the Cappadocians, and now Pope Leo of Rome was added to this canonical list of trustworthy names, at which time a Greek translation of his *Tome* was read to all present. While there was some fear that a new confession of faith would make the Church look like she had to redefine things every few decades, and despite some opposition to Leo's *Tome*, the Council of Chalcedon ended with general acclamation from the bishops present who chanted, "Peter has spoken through Leo. . . . Why was this not read at Ephesus? Dioscorus concealed it from us." In mid-October of 451, then, Dioscorus of Alexandria was deposed (with wild rumors circulating of his being an adulterer and even a murderer) and duly exiled, dying sick and alone just a few years later.

Twenty-seven canons emerged from these months of debate and deliberation. In the end, 452 signatures confirmed the Christology of Leo in the presence of Marcian and Pulcheria, who were here deemed a "new Constantine" and a "new Helena." However, upset with the twenty-eighth canon which declared Constantinople to be "the New Rome," Leo was less than satisfied with the results of Chalcedon, even withholding his official ratification of the conciliar proceedings, despite his victory over Eutyches. Leo pointed out that the canons attached to these proceedings never made their way back to Rome. He therefore acknowledged that Constantinople was an imperially consecrated city important in all affairs political and civil, but that did not make it an apostolic see: "Let the city of Constantinople have its glory and under the protecting hand of

God, may it long enjoy your Clemency's rule. Nevertheless, things secular and things religious do not have the same basis; nothing erected is going to be stable apart from that Rock which the Lord placed in its foundation."[131]

This was written the same year Atilla the Hun invaded Italy, bravely met outside the city walls of Rome by Pope Leo. While modern day historians debate the reason, shortly after this encounter, Atilla unexplainedly retreats and leaves Italy. What was said, what was discussed, what was traded, we do not know; we only know that the presence of this holy man turned back a marauding army in the world, just as his wisdom and prayerfulness helped put an end to heresy and division in the Church. Pope Leo died peacefully in Rome on November 10, 461, and his body is able to be visited on the Vatican Hill to this day near the tomb of St. Peter, the apostle whom he emulated and with whom he has been eternally associated.

Successors of St. Peter

Leo's pontificate made it clear to the world that the see of Rome must be held supreme in safeguarding the purity of the Faith. When the council fathers declared at Chalcedon that "Peter has spoken through Leo, Peter has spoken through Leo; this is what we believe, this is the faith of Christ's Apostles," they were not inventing doctrine but voicing a long-held belief that, somehow, Peter's apostolic see had a certain primacy over all the other ancient dioceses

---

[131] Leo the Great to Marcian (May 22, 452), *Letter* 104; trans. Hunt, *op. cit.*, p. 179.

throughout the world. What this primacy meant in actual practice remains contentious today, but we see from some of the earliest testimonies, the ancient Church looked to Rome for guidance and definitive answers in matters of doctrine. That is not to say that Rome always acted appropriately, often overstepping boundaries and protocol, but no Church history is complete without looking at how the Rock of Peter's primacy developed and was experienced throughout the Christian world.

So, as we conclude this brief history, we return to the more magnificent book that recorded our beginnings: "And I tell you, you are Peter, and on this rock I will build my church, and the powers of death shall not prevail against it" (Mt 16:18). Where is the contest? A rock against a gate? Christ has already won this fight for us, the one, true Rock who outlasts all false promises, all false messiahs. How effective is a gate in a battle? Gates only work when one chooses to go through them. The enemy has no power which we do not freely give over, and that is why he has to twist the good to make evil look somehow attractive, somehow promising, but that scintilla of goodness which is in every sinful pursuit lasts only for a time, always disappointing after the thrill is over.

But this is where the gift of discernment fortifies that earlier gift of free will. But we are not left to our own wits and limited wisdom. We have been incorporated into the mind of Jesus Christ, and it is in the apostles where we most safely and surely secure that mind. That is what Peter ultimately represents and even offers: the true union of hearts and minds in Christ. This is the gift Jesus promises his Body and that is what Leo preached with his life, the unity of true religion. Leo thus writes to the bishops over in the province of Vienne: "The Lord desired that the dispensing of this gift should be shared as a task by all the Apostles, but in such a way that he put the principal charge on the most blessed Peter, the highest of all the Apostles. He wanted his gifts to flow into the entire body from Peter himself, as it were from the head."[132]

Peter is listed always at the head of any apostolic list in the New Testament; within that college of twelve, he is recorded as the head and proves to be the one who represents the others—e.g., "he appeared to Cephas, then to the twelve" (1 Cor 15:5). Even the unbounded St. Paul makes sure he "went up to Jerusalem to confer with Cephas" (Gal 1:18). No other list of bishops is as carefully recorded as is that of the Diocese of Rome in the early Church. While there are gaps and holes in the lists of the Dioceses of Jerusalem and Antioch, Alexandria and Constantinople in those early years, the popes of Rome are meticulously listed because something more was expected of these who followed St. Peter.

This is not to say that the Church's structure was as clearly unified around Peter from the start. There were disparate communities, and the bigger diocesan sees competed for primacy and most often did not even bother with one another when inconvenient. But as early as the late first century we saw how Clement of Rome began to instruct the communities of the East when to date the celebration

---

[132] Leo the Great, *Letter* 10; trans. Hunt, *op. cit.*, p. 37.

of Easter. As the living Peter, the bishop of Rome was the universal adjudicator of dogma and often of discipline as well. This is why the Church historian Eusebius looks at Pope Victor (189–99) only a century later and sees one who judged heresy and acted for the sake of true ecclesial unity. Against Gnostic sects who wanted to interpret the Christian faith in their own novel way, Pope Victor insisted that unless a community was in union with his office, they were to be cast aside: "Thereupon Victor, head of the Roman church, attempted at one stroke to cut off from the common unity all the Asian dioceses, together with the neighbouring churches, on the ground of heterodoxy, and pilloried them in letters in which he announced the total excommunication of all his fellow-Christians there."[133]

By the third century, the Chair of Peter had become a symbol of the unity Christ intended for all of his followers. The word for this chair in both Greek and Latin is *cathedra*, from which our word "cathedral" comes, the bishop's main parish in any one diocese, symbolizing Catholic unity with the one ultimate *cathedra* in Rome, the Chair of Peter. The bishop of Carthage, the future saint and martyr, Cyprian could proclaim with authority not only that the Lord told Peter, "thou art Peter and upon this rock I will build my Church," but also:

> He founded a single chair [*cathedra*], thus establishing by His own authority the source and hallmark of the Church's oneness. No doubt the others were all

---

133   Eusebius, *The History of the Church*, Bk. 5.24; trans. Williamson, *op. cit.*, p. 172.

that Peter was, but a primacy is given to Peter, and it is thus made clear that there is but one Church and one Chair. So, too, even if they are all shepherds, we are shown but one flock which is to be fed by all the Apostles in common accord. If a man does not hold fast to this oneness of Peter, does he imagine that he still holds the faith? If he deserts the Chair of Peter upon whom the Church was built, has he still confidence that he is in the Church?[134]

Like Cyprian, the best of the Church Fathers knew that their community, their diocese, never had the last word. They knew that they were called to live and pray and profess the Faith in a universal and unified voice. The biblical images used to capture this desired harmony were all based on the trustworthiness and the solidity of Simon Peter's faith above all (Rock, *Petra*), on his preeminent ability to set prisoners free (keys, *claves*), and upon the needed unity symbolized by his *cathedra* of unity.

This latter image becomes more and more important as the decades unfold and the diocesan structure takes more tasks upon itself as the Roman Empire falls and the rise of states and nations begins, putting the Church in a more obvious need for visible unity. Early in this process, Optatus of Milevus (d. 397), a Numidian bishop, linked this symbolic chair with Christ's changing Simon's name to the Rock: "You cannot deny that you are aware that in the city of Rome the episcopal chair was given first to Peter; the chair

---

[134] Cyprian, *On the Unity of the Church* §4 (1st edition); trans. Bévenot, *op. cit.*, pp. 46–47.

in which Peter sat, the same who was head—that is why he is also called Cephas or Rock—of all the apostles; the one chair in which unity is maintained by all." And around this same time, Pope Damasus (d. 384) decreed "that the holy Roman Church has been placed at the forefront not by the conciliar decisions of other churches, but has received the primacy by the evangelic voice of our Lord and Savior, who says: 'You are Peter, and upon this rock I will build my Church, and the gates of hell will not prevail against it; and I will give to you the keys of the kingdom of heaven ...' The first see, therefore, is that of Peter the apostle, that of the Roman Church, which has neither stain nor blemish nor anything like it."[135]

The early Church saw in Peter the divine mandate from Christ himself to know and follow his own heavenly teaching. In allowing Christ to enter and thus take up his own life in ours is much more than doctrinal orthodoxy, but it is more, not less. Intellectual and devotional surrender must occur if we are going to let Christ live our lives. We must resist thinking we know better than the apostles and the saints, we must cease thinking that the two-thousand-year-old Magisterium is out of touch with modern struggles. In striving to conform my thoughts and opinions to the mind of Christ's Church as expressed in the fidelity of Sacred

---

[135] *Decree of Damasus* §3; trans. William Jurgens, *The Faith of the Early Fathers* (Collegeville, MN: The Liturgical Press, 1970), p. 406. This is another wonderful (3-volme) series containing primary citations from the Church Fathers. These quotes cover the years from the Apostolic Fathers up to the early seventh century, and as insightful and helpful as these volumes are, the selected quotes are unfortunately often simply one or two lines.

Tradition, I can begin to think and understand, to counsel and ultimately to love like Jesus himself. He longs to unite my heart and mind to his, and it begins with the sense of trust that he and his Church are one sacred Person.

In one way, the office of Peter is a sacrament that makes a past reality present today. As the Eucharist provides us the incarnate Lord—Body and Blood, Soul and Divinity—making the sacrifice of Calvary and the joy of Easter efficacious for us today, the papal ministry makes real Peter's confession of faith and Jesus's consequent entrusting of his one true Church to him even two thousand years later:

> Divine assistance is also given to the successors of the apostles, teaching in communion with the successor of Peter, and, in a particular way, to the bishop of Rome, pastor of the whole Church, when, without arriving at an infallible definition and without pronouncing in a "definitive manner," they propose in the exercise of the ordinary Magisterium a teaching that leads to better understanding of Revelation in matters of faith and morals. To this ordinary teaching the faithful "are to adhere . . . with religious assent" (Vatican II's *Lumen Gentium* §25) which, though distinct from the assent of faith, is nonetheless an extension of it.[136]

In offering one's opinions to Mother Church, the faithful Christian seeks and is able to think with the mind of Christ. As Chesterton knew for himself and expressed so challengingly for us, the Catholic Church is the only way

---

[136] CCC §892.

of life "that frees a man from the degrading slavery of being a child of his age." The torrents of this world are swift and shallow. We see in our own day how each passing fad and popular trend sweeps those looking for meaning and purpose into a place where they eventually lose even their own selves.

As one who freely enters into this great story of Christ's sacred Body, though, I can be assured that my life's story becomes his. Only here can my days have ultimate meaning. As a faithful follower of two thousand years of Christian teaching and not just a dabbler in those parts of the Gospel that I happen to like, I am assured that it is no longer I who live at the center of my worldview and value system, but it is now Christ who lives—and thus thinks and feels—in me. This is why faithful Catholics think and live differently on such counter cultural issues as the indissoluble marriage of a man and a woman, the beauty of new life and the ugliness of artificial birth control and abortion, on the dignity of refugees, migrant workers, and the forgotten whom only the Church knows will be first in the Kingdom of God. Yet that kingdom is not some distant reality. The Kingdom of God is Christ alive in every human soul, manifested by a way of life inaugurated here through Christ's founding of his Church. This is why I can trust the bishop of Rome and the teachings that flow through this two millennial office, because Christ is the One who has placed him there, wanting his own right judgment and revelation to be understood properly by fallible minds like our own.

This is why Church history matters, as the continuation of what began in Bethlehem—namely, the tangibly incarnate and historically concrete mind of God himself. If the Church is regarded simply as a keeper of rules or relics, just another human institution, the Church has no more authority or significance than any other social assemblage. But happily that is not the case. The Church is not a façade but a face, and that is why Christians have referred to the Church as their Mother since the third century. This is also why all the Church councils we have looked at here coalesce into the faces of Mary and Jesus. Without Mary, the divine would have remained an other-worldly transcendent Being, glimpsed perhaps still everywhere, but because of Mary's yes, God can now be found somewhere. This is the heart of the Incarnation: the enfleshed presence of God desirous of union with particular, concrete others. This is how he loves us each personally and uniquely in a way that pure spirit cannot—he now calls us friends (Jn 15:5). He can now speak to us face to face, he can feed us and even be fed by us (Mt 25:31–40). Without Mary, dogma and doctrine would have remained ethereal and abstract, but as with the Son of God himself, she instantiates and makes concrete in time and space the Truth of God. This is why God came to earth; this is why he founded a Church.

Conclusion

Imagine: Forty days of fasting and abstinence are now drawing to a close. It is the Mass of the Easter Vigil, sometime around the year 400, and a bishop (perhaps Ephiphanius of Cyprus, the heretic hunter who died in 403) mounts a raised platform to preach on Christ's descent from the cross into the depths of the underworld. The listeners in this shadowy cathedral are thus brought back to the movements of that first Holy Saturday centuries ago. The homily is characteristically Oriental, surely delivered by a bishop, surely preached in Greek. It likens the Christian story to a shepherd going after his sheep, it is classically liturgical in tone, and it emphasizes the divine descent of the New Adam as he seeks to incorporate all children of the first Adam and Eve into his life-giving death:

> Something strange is happening. There is a great silence on earth today, a great silence and stillness. The whole earth keeps silence because the King is asleep. . . . He has to search for our first parent, as for a lost sheep. . . . The Lord approached Adam and Eve, bearing the cross, the weapon that had won him the victory. At the sight of him Adam, the first man he had created, struck his breast in terror and cried out: "The Lord be with you." Christ answered him, "And with your spirit." He then took him by the hand and raised him up, saying, "Sleeper, awake, and rise from the dead, and Christ will give you light. Out of love for you and for your descendants I now by my own authority command all who are held in bondage to come forth, all who are in darkness to be enlightened, all who are sleeping: Arise! I order you, O sleeper, awake! I did not create you to be held a prisoner in hell. Rise from the dead, for I am the life of the dead. Rise up, work of my hands, you who were created in my image. Rise, let us leave this place, for you are in

> me and I am in you, and together we form only one
> person and we can never again be separated.[137]

What makes this Holy Saturday homily so illuminating is the paradoxical intrigue that Christ is more committed to Adam's eternal salvation than Adam is.

This is the God of the Chosen People, a God who is faithful even when, especially when, his beloved turns away. We see this pursuit cast in a liturgical tone: "May the Lord be with you," "And with your spirit." And where does this pursuit take place? In the depths and in the darkness of one's own hell. This is where Christ descends to meet Adam, to meet every one of us. That is, there is nothing in any Christian's life that turns this thirsty and thankful God away from his children. He is the Almighty Creator who for our sake has become our Crucified Lord, and he continues to do whatever he can to woo and to win us over to him.

This invitation results not just in my or your salvation but the salvation of all who respond to it. Christ founded a Church so he could save not individuals only, but members of a family. That Christ founded a visible Church, no ancient Christian denied. Where and how that Church was founded, most agreed. This is the sole and unmatchable Church which herself alone enjoys "that tradition derived from the apostles, of the very great, the very ancient, and universally known Church founded and organized at Rome

---

[137] The author of (what is referred to) this *Ancient Holy Saturday Homily* remains unknown, although often it is ascribed to Epiphanius of Salamis (d. 403). There are many translations (the original is found at PG 43.439-63), but the best English translation is found at http://www.vatican.va/spirit/documents/spirit_20010414_omelia-sabato-santo_en.html.

by the two most glorious apostles, Peter and Paul; as also [by pointing out] the faith preached to men, which comes down to our time by means of the successions of the bishops. For it is a matter of necessity that every Church should agree with this Church, on account of its preeminent authority [*potiorem principalitatem*]."[138]

Rome was thus honored as preeminent from Christianity's start, not because of the power of bloodthirsty emperors but because of the fidelity of the bloodied apostles. That blood continues to be poured out on every Catholic altar and in every Christian act of martyrdom. This is the story of God's faithful people since the time of Abel and those prophets persecuted for the sake of the one true God. This is the story of Jesus Christ and his Church. This is our story.

---

[138] Irenaeus, *Against Heresies*, 3.3.2; trans. A. Cleveland Coxe, *Ante-Nicene Fathers*, *op. cit.*, p. 415.